ON A JOURNEY WITH JESUS

Poems in times of joy and despair

RHODA MOULDING

Kingdom Publishers

On a Journey with Jesus
Poems in times of joy and despair

Copyright © Rhoda Moulding 2019

All rights reserved. No part of this book may be reproduced in any form by photocopying or any electronic or mechanical means, including information storage or retrieval systems, without permission in writing from both the copyright owner and the publisher of the book. The right of Rhoda Moulding to be identified as the author of this work has been asserted by her in accordance with the Copyright, Designs and Patents Act 1988 and any subsequent amendments thereto.
A catalogue record for this book is available from the British Library.

ISBN: 978-1-913247-02-7

1st Edition 2019 by Kingdom Publishers
Kingdom Publishers
London, UK.

Dedicated

To Deborah, Laurie and a mum,
My mother, daughter and our son,
Separation has undone,
What we had when life began,
Heart aches hard to overcome,
Yet Christ remains our faithful one.

Preface

A lot happened in my first eleven years. Until the age of seven I had been brought up in a children's home in Bournemouth along with my brother before being taken to live with parents we hardly knew.

At the age of seven, I permanently lost the use of my right hand in an accident; since then, I had to adapt myself to the use of just one workable hand.

At the age of eleven, we moved to London; it was there that my father was killed trying to stop a brawl outside a public house.

Later I was surprised to be introduced to a step sister I never knew I had.

We were made homeless during the London blitz after the house we were living suffered a direct hit while we were under ground shelter on Wandsworth Common.

Now homeless, we were taken to live with grandparents I never knew existed. All this in my first eleven years.

When first we arrived at my grandparents' house I discovered they attended a small church gathering which was a subdivision of a universal movement whose ruling principle was complete separation from the world. For instance, You could not eat, drink, marry or live in the same house as those not in the same fellowship. You could not attend another church other than theirs, all this along with many, many more rules and regulations; in the case these rules were not met, excommunication from church would take place.

While at my grandparents', I discovered that my mother had a child out of wedlock; as a result, she had been excommunicated from the church, which made her run away to London leaving the child with her parents. There she met my father, got married and had my brother and I, but owing to circumstances, she was unable to keep us and we were put into care; when I was eight months and my brother when he was three months old.

Now here we were living with our grandparents and were made to attend their church, taking on and believing their doctrines over the next thirty nine years; being taught that we were the only Christian church that was pleasing God by keeping their rules and doctrines. I met and married John, who shared the same belief, and we had five children.

Over those years I saw many members of my family excommunicated from the church, which meant that that person was completely cut off from the family and would have to leave the home with no contact with family and friends whatsoever.

For instance, five years after meeting my sister for the first time she was excommunicated when she was seventeen for marrying someone outside the fellowship so I never saw her over the following thirty-three years.

Later John's parents, brother and sister were expelled from the fellowship; we met them again twenty-one years later. Then my brother was excommunicated and we lost touch for ten years.

The worst was yet to come when my husband and eldest son were expelled, which meant they had to leave the house or I had to, They had to live in a caravan, while I was under strict instructions not to have contact with them or I would be expelled too and I knew if that was so, I would have had the rest of my children taken from me to live with other members of the sect.

I struggled on without my husband and son for four years. The pain was so unbearable at times that I had thoughts of taking my own life. The universal leader of the Sect insisted his ministry had to be read before anything else. As a mother with four children at home I had no time to read his booklets that came out every week as well as the Bible, so I stopped reading his booklets and delved deeper into the Bible.

The more I read, the more I became convinced I had not been taught the true nature of God; He did not appear to me to be as hard and legal as I had imagined Him.

Then as I was reading 1 Corinthians 7 (I will leave you to read it) I began to realise my place was with my husband. I mentioned this chapter to my 18-year-old son, his answer to this was, "If I carried on, I would find myself out of fellowship ". I knew from that moment on that I had to keep my thoughts to myself.

Now with no one to talk about my concerns it was just God and my Bible.

I was in turmoil wanting to do what was right before God. It is hard to decide when, from an early age, you have been taught to think in a certain way with such strict beliefs; I became ill both mentally and physically as I knew I had to make a decision whether to stay with the sect or to leave. I knew that if I left, they would take my children to live with other members of the sect.

I escaped when the house was empty, the two eldest at work and my mother asleep in her granny's flat; I took with me the two youngest children aged eight and nine and I left to join my husband.

John took us away for a week; when we returned we found the house empty. Our two eldest children and my mother had left the house to live with other members of the fellowship.

The first few poems were written to God telling Him my heart ached, pain and sorrow of having to separate from those I loved so much, while others were written at the joy and surprise of discovering the true nature of God.

Years have rolled on but we are still denied contact with our children and grandchildren.

When writing these poems, I had no intentions of having them published, for as you read them you will find that most of them are personal experiences, concerns and prayers shared with God, mainly through those difficult times expressed in my testimony on page 4; however, I was advised to share these experiences as a way to help others showing that these fruits are not only for the glory of God, but also for our own spiritual growth through personal suffering.

Content

1.	The Valley Of Tears	1
2.	Happiness	3
3.	A Song Within My Heart	5
4.	I Am God's Possession	7
5.	Church Anniversary	9
6.	My Church	10
7.	The Window Of Promise	12
8.	Psalm 63	14
9.	Lord, What Is Man?	16
10.	Psalm 139	18
11	I'm In Christ And He's In Me.	20
12.	The Father's Delight Is In Jesus	22
13.	Low I Stand At The Door And Knock	24
14.	Mercy And Grace	26
15.	His Humility	28
16.	Just A Kiss	30
17.	This Is My Mountain	31
18.	Thoughts Of Paradise	32
19.	Paradise With Me	33
20.	Free Forgiveness	35
21.	Isaiah 53	37
22.	Passing By	38
23.	The Empty Tomb	40
24.	Because Christ Lives	42
25.	As A Child In The London Blitz	43
26.	Christmas In The Forties	45
27.	The Pharisee	47
28.	Eden	49
29.	Speaking Of Kings	51
30.	Was It By Chance?	53
31.	One Denomination	56
32.	Joseph	58
33.	No Room	60
34.	The Truth Of Christmas	61
35.	Where Is He?	62
36.	The Gift	63

Content

37. The Census	64
38. The World's Creator Comes To Earth	64
39. The Heavenly Story	65
40. Shepherd's Speak	65
41. Wise Men	66
42. The Christmas Story	67
43. Your Ways Are Not My Ways	69
44. Don't Be A Blob	71
45. Trust In The Lord	73
46. Seek The Lord While He May Be Found	75
47. Religious Religions	78
48. The Master Painter	80
49. Who Is This Man?	82
50. Tales Repeatedly Told	84
51. Poor Albert	86
52. The Man With The Light	90
53. Father's Day	93
54. Abandoned Morals	95
55. God Looks On The Inward	97
56. British Weather	99
57. Chasing Bubbles	101
58. A Mother's Concern	104
59. The Full Armour Of God	106
60. Breast Plate Righteousness	107
61. Helmet of Salvation	107
62. Shield of Faith	108
63. The Belt of Truth	108
64. The Sward of The Spirit	109
65. The Web Of Lies	110
66. The Good Samaritan	113
67. Self-righteousness	115
68. See What Women Can Do	117
69. Leprosy	119
70. The Master's Touch	120
71. There Was A Proud Man	121
72. Lazarus And The Rich Man	122

THE VALLEY OF TEARS

*This, at that time, was a cry to God to
help me through the pain of bereavement
after being denied access to my mother
and two children who themselves had
to adhere to the rules of the church as regards
complete separation from the world,
believing, as I once did, that their church's
demands were justifiable and that complete
separation was the only way to please Christ*

The Valley of Tears

I stand in the valley, the valley of tears,
Calling my God, who's the Ancient of years,
He say's I'm his child, it will all work for good,
And all in his presence will be understood,
Reflecting life's sorrows one day will I see,
This road that I tread God had planned it for me?

It's hard to hold on when my faith is so weak,
Strengthen me now, Lord, your presence I seek,
O God of all ages, O God of my past,
O God of my future on thee I am cast,
Bring joy in my darkness and peace in this storm,
Hold me and keep me with hope for the dawn.

My Shepherd and Saviour, my Guide and my God,
Let me bend to your will, your staff and your rod,
Bring light to my way as I walk through the dark,
With a sense of your love that will lighten my heart,
Let me feel, let me know that your still at my side,
Let your peace overcome all this hurt that's inside.

Shine a light in my darkness; bring peace to my pain,
Show me your presence; come closer again,
Roll back the clouds that your face may appear,
Or a touch of your hand to prove you are near,
A beacon of hope, a word from your throne,
Prove I'm wrapped in your arms and I don't walk alone.

Help me to trust you, to trust in your love,
To feel you are near not remote far above,
Though waters are raging they will not consume,
Through rejection and sadness, please, see I reach home,
Show me your promises, trusted and sure,
Hold me and keep me and help me endure.

Then let me praise through the height of the storm,
Though mingled with sadness let joy be reborn,
Let me walk through this valley accepting your will,
Knowing you love me and walk with me still,
Help me remember, each crisis in life,
Your presence, Lord Jesus, will always suffice.

HAPPINESS

*I started writing this in self- pity
while trying to recover from a bout of flu.
My husband John was out of
work, and, as usual, the ache in my heart
for our absent children. As I was writing, it was as if God said,
"True happiness will not be found in self-pity but serving me
and my people, reaching out with what you have learnt
in all this and use it to help others."*

Happiness

O Happiness, where art thou found?
My self-pursuits prove hollow ground,
I seek thee as they seek the wind,
Reach out but nothing in the end,
As laughter round my world surrounds
It echoes back an empty sound.

In self pursuit my eyes I cast,
In hope of finding you at last,
Then when I think you're in my grasp,
In fleeting moments, you have passed,
And then again comes back the sound,
O happiness where art thou found.

O happiness, where art thou found,
When storms of life push me around,
I turn to Him, who lives on high,
O heavenly Father, hear my cry,
I heard a still small voice within,
Say, "Happiness is serving Him".

I turn to see, a face I scan
A face marred more than any man,
His head, I saw a crown of thorn,
His flesh was scarred where whips had worn,
His hands showed holes the nails had born,
And feet the wooded cross had torn.

All this He said "I did for thee
Have you done anything for me?"
Had I done anything for Him?
He, who died my soul to win?
And here I am, I'm taken in,
What selfish pity lie within?

O Lord, how selfish can I be?
How blind my eye that did not see,
O Lord, your voice has turned me round,
Not self but serving Christ I'm bound,
While He my heart with joy has crowned,
And shown where happiness is found.

A SONG WITHIN MY HEART

There are times, while under pressure, we feel God
miles away you want his presence but it seems you can't Reach Him.
On this occasion I had
To ask myself "why, after all I was going through
could I not reach God?" I was made to realise this
distance was of my own making, I had been so wrapped
up in self-pity that my eyes wandered off the One who takes
our sorrows and carry our burdens.

A Song Within My Heart

Oh I was feeling wretched as I lay in bed with flu,
While housework and the washing were pilling up to do,
Husband looking for a job and bills we had to pay,
And the loss of family loved ones that hurt me every day.

Lord, I need your presence, draw near me if you will,
Lift this heavy heart of mine and say, Lord, "Peace, be still".
Come, calm these troubled waters that rip my soul apart,
Saviour, come thou quickly and put a song within my heart.

"A song within your heart" God said "but child, you're never still,
You spend so many hours a day just working out your will,
Your prayers are repetitions and your love has lost its glow,
Your burdens and your sorrows are hard to bear I know

"Lay them on my shoulders, child, and let me take the pain,
I'll guide you through the desert storm so you can sing again
I know you feel rejected by those you used to walk ,
But I could make you sing again if you and I could talk".

To sing again, to sing again, how can this ever be?
With darkness all around me, your face I cannot see,
Can you return my children? Can I see them coming home,
When my price for Christian freedom was to leave them on their own?

And now I know not how to sing or how to praise in song,
Or what is true or what is false or what church to belong,
Oh guide me, Saviour, through the storm while others turn away,
Teach me how to learn from you, be thou my rock I pray.

Then did I hear the Saviour say, "The road is hard, I know
While others may reject you, I will not let you go,
And all those months you've laboured I've looked on you in love,
Come, let me lift your broken heart to heavenly realms above."

It was then my spirit lifted, it was all I need to know,
That through life's pain He loves me and will not let me go,
It was as if the hand of Jesus drew back the darkening shroud,
And bought me up beside Him and we sat above the cloud.

Above the clouds with Jesus? Yes, we sat above life's woe,
With Him above my sorrows, both looking down below,
We could hear the thunder rolling and in it had my part,
But I'm looking down with Jesus a song within my heart.

I AM GOD'S POSSESSION

Ephesians1: 13- 14
And you also were also included in Christ
when you heard the message of truth, the
gospel of salvation. When you believed, you
were marked in him with a seal, the promise
Holy Spirit, who is a deposit guaranteeing
our inheritance and until the redemption of
those who are God's possession - to the praise
of his glory.

I find that such a comfort just to think that every believer in Christ Jesus is God's possession and whatever trial we go through we are not our own but God's possession.

I Am God's Possession

The day that I believed the promise of God's Word,
The day that I accepted God's Christ to be my Lord,
He sealed me with his Spirit, so I am marked as His,
A guaranteed deposit makes me assured of this,
That I am his possession,
He's claimed me as his own,
And hand in hand together,
We walk the journey home.

And though at times the road gets rough,
As heavenward I am bound,
A little pressure from his hand assures me He's around,
And when I get despondent and hurt along the way,
With both his arms he holds me and softly He will say,
"You are my possession,
I've claimed you as my own,
And hand in hand together,
We walk the journey home".

Christ is my salvation; He is everything to me,
It's through his blood I'm purchased into his family,
His blood is on my lintel while the angel passes by,
I will live with Him forever and here's the reason why,
For I am God's possession,
He claimed me as his own,
And hand in hand together,
We walk the journey home.

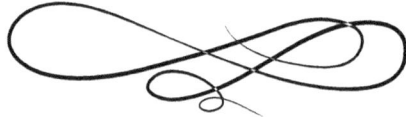

CHURCH ANNIVERSARY & MY CHURCH

*After feeling the pain of rejection and
the experience from our former church,
imagine our joy at being led to this one.
I can only explain in the following two poems
just how much comfort and healing took
place within me.
God knew what we needed and provided*

Church Anniversary

Church Anniversary. Is it yours as well?
Have you a story like to mine to tell?
When first you enter here, can you review?
How much this church since then has meant to you?

For I remember well the day I came,
And faces still I see that I could name,
Timidly we entered, bruised and shaking,
Battered by the storm, our hearts were breaking.

Loved ones lost, no sight of restoration,
But here it was, God met our devastation.
For in this church, we found so great a treasure,
A love we never thought would be our measure.

Not in the sermon or the preacher's word,
But in the things unspoken that we heard,
The gentleness of Christ was so revealed
Through those who in this church his Spirit sealed.

And I, from brethren's background still recall,
In Bible teaching, thought I knew it all,
But here was something I could not explain,
I knew nothing and must start again.

Though many years have passed yet still I see,
The love in here that first attracted me,
A church that meets and prays for one another,
And hold you as they would a natural brother.

My Church

My church is like a haven,
Where ships limp home from sea,
And stormtorn vessels come to rest
In God's vicinity,
With weary tales and battered sales,
Renewing strength that never fails.

My church is like Adullam,
The cave where David dwells,
where lame and poor and thirsty
Can drink from springing wells,
Where thirst is quenched and fear dispensed,
And song and dancing have commenced.

My church is like the upper room,
Where songs of praise are heard,
And Jesus comes to join us
As promised in his Word,
Where love descends and praise ascends,
To Him who greets us all as friends.

My church is like a nesting place,
Where I can keep my young,
To nurture with the precious Word,
As soon as life began,
To learn his ways from early days,
And follow, serve and seek his ways.

My church is built of people,
That God has gathered in,
Where we are all one family,
And deemed his next of kin,
And there we share the Father's care
With all that come to worship there.

My church, my Lord, is all I need,
Along the narrow way,
That leads me to my Father's throne,
That I shall reach one day,
Oh blessed hope, that scene beyond,
My soul is there sufficed,
United with the one whole church,
To be the bride of Christ.

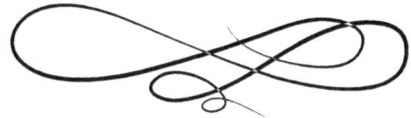

THE WINDOW OF PROMISE

*While visiting a church in Wales, I was struck
by the beauty of the stained-glass window,
the sun shone through it so radiantly. Although
I couldn't see the other side of the stained glass,
It made me think of the promises that eye has
not seen or ear heard that lie behind a window
which we cannot look through but God
has already prepared for those who love Him.*

The Window of Promise

As I look through the window of promise,
And taste of the fruit that it brings,
Then my hope is alive for the future,
To live with the King of kings.

As I look through the window of promise,
What wonders are filling my eyes,
I can't wait for the day of fulfillment,
When I see Him descend from the skies.

As I look through the window of promise,
Each time seeing more than before,
There's no end to the fortunes of heaven,
To the faithful who strive to endure.

Take a look through the window of promise,
Our hope through God's word is made sure,
Bright colours from glory shine stronger,
As each time you look you see more.

So Christian, through faith persevering,
Your goal to the heavenly shores,
What you see through the window of promise,
Overcomer, one day will be yours.

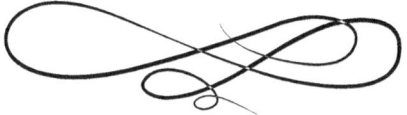

A PSALM OF DAVID'S

Written from Psalm 63.

O God, you are my God
My soul will cling to you,
And trust you through the storms of life,
Till you have bought me through.

A Psalm of David's

O God, you are my God,
You earnestly I seek,
For in this dry and weary land,
Your hand my soul doth keep.

O God, you are my God,
Better than life your love,
And all my days your name proclaim,
All other names above.

O God, you are my God,
In a dry and thirsty land,
You satisfy my soul with food
Provided by your hand.

I remember in my bed,
In the stillness darkness brings,
How your right hand upholdeth me,
In the shadow of your wings.

O God, you are my God,
My soul will cling to you,
And trust you through the storms of life,
'Till you have bought me through.

Through to that glorious day,
When conflict will be 'or,
And I shall know as I am known,
On Canaan's blissful shore.

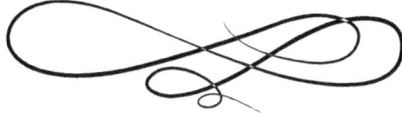

Lord, what is man?

Lord, what is man that thou art mindful of him?
We have to wonder as David did when he asked
God that question.

Lord, What is Man?

Lord, what is man that thou art mindful of him?
The sons of men bound with the weight of sin,
That though, O Lord, in all you glorious splendour,
Should bend so low in love our hearts to win?

O who am I that you are mindful of me?
A son of earth that thou should with me be,
I did no deed to warrant your attention,
I had no fame or name that one could mention.

Born in sin along with all the nation,
No thought of God in all my contemplation,
But yet you thought of me, Oh, why? Oh, why?
Should you extend your love to such as I?

I stand amazed before your throne of grace,
Absorbed in wonder by your loves embrace,
That I, considered worthy through your son,
To have a part in what your Christ has done.

I love you Lord, what more is there to say,
But fill me with this love, Lord, every day,
A love that overflows to saturation,
And fill my heart to praise in adoration.

PSALM 139

Where can I run from his presence?
Where can I hide from his face?
What kind of relationship do I have with God?
Do I run toward Him or run from Him?
Do I embrace his ways with me or do I rebel?
Even in taught times He has only my good at heart.
It would be an uncaring God to give me all I wanted,
How would I grow in his likeness or
develop in character or be available
to help others if I was not disciplined?

Psalm 139

Where can I run from his presence?
Where can I hide from his face?
Where can I shield from his watchful eye?
Where can I find such a place?

If I go to the highest mountain,
Or down to the deepest sea,
Even down to the depth of the earth,
My Maker can still see me,

I say surely the darkness will hide me,
And the light become night around
Even the darkness will not be dark,
There is no where I cannot be found.

But why should I hide from his presence?
Why should I run from his face?
Or take myself from his watchful eye,
Or some other hiding place.

When my sins Jesus said are forgiven,
I am free because He took my place,
God's wrath for my sins, Jesus took it all,
So why should I hide from his face.

It's the sinner, who runs from his presence,
Shuns the road that the Saviour once trod,
It's the man, who rejects God's salvation,
That is seeking to hide from his face.

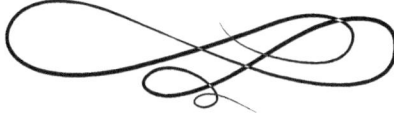

I'M IN CHRIST AND HE'S IN ME

*Father, just as you are in me I am in you,
may they also be in us so that the world
may believe that you have sent me that they
may be one as we are one, I in them and
you in me. may they be bought to complete
unity to let the world know that you have
sent me and has loved them as you have
loved me.
John 17:21-23.*

I'm In Christ And He's In Me

I in Him and He in me,
I am amazed that one could be
Bone of his bone, flesh of his flesh,
And all in Christ I can possess,
Yes, Christ is mine and I am his,
What bought about such grace as this?

I live in Him, what grace I see,
Not only that, He lives in me,
I but a sinner saved by grace,
Once hellward bound by Adam's race,
Yet in his Word I plainly see,
That I'm in Christ and He's in me.

Now features seen in Him I see,
I should display if He's in me,
My every part is ownd by Him,
Because his Spirit lives within,
His love, his truth, his gentleness,
Are attributes I should posses.

I live in Him, my greatest gain,
The King of kings my life sustains,
I live in Him, O love divine,
All in Him, his sonship's mine,
I live in Him, what joy, what bliss,
God said "you're mine" because of this.

He lives in me, I live in Him,
My cup o'er flows beyond the brim,
O mystery that God should plan,
Such nearness to his creature man,
To take us from our sinful state,
And with himself through Christ relate.

That to the highest heights above,
Before his throne divine his love,
Would me, a sinner, saved by grace,
Give me through Christ a sonship's place,
O love divine, how can this be?
That I'm in Christ and He's in me.

Through years of sadness now I see,
I'm not alone for Christ's in me,
And I'm in Him, my sorrows his,
He said "you must remember this,
We cannot separated be,
As I'm in you and you're in me."

So we walk as one together,
Share a bond beyond all measure,
He strengthens me for I'm possessed,
By Christ that wants my very best,
My sorrows shared, how can this be?
Cos I'm in Christ and He's in me.

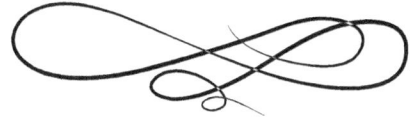

*THE FATHERS DELIGHT IS
IN JESUS*

*And a voice came from heaven.
"You are my Son whom I love,
with you I am well pleased."
Luke 3:22.*

The Father's Delight is In Jesus

The Father's delight is in Jesus,
And those that his love has secured,
The fruit that his love has accomplished,
Through the pain and the suffering endured.

The Father's delight is in Jesus,
Those plans God invested in Him,
Were fulfilled to the very last detail,
When He lay down his life for our sin.

The Father's delight is in Jesus,
When the heavens saw Jesus depart,
To come down from the heights of his glory,
To reveal to the nations God's heart.

The Father's delight is in Jesus,
And He loves us to tell of his worth,
To God it's a sweet smelling odour,
His life of obedience on earth.

The Father's delight is in Jesus,
Let us tell of his glory and fame,
How He bought about our salvation,
And made us God's sons through his name.

The Father's delight is in Jesus,
And in us if we live like his son,
So let's walk in the steps of the Saviour,
Delighting the Father as one.

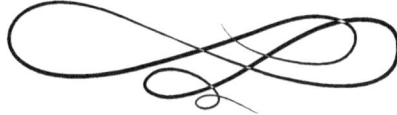

LOW I STAND AT THE DOOR AND KNOCK

"Low I stand at the door and knock if anyone should hear my voice I will come in and sup with him."

This text affected me as a child at the age of nine. I was at a Christian camp, never having heard the gospel before; when this Scripture was read, it all seemed so simple, I had only to let Christ into my heart.

I said the prayer to myself and felt immediately uplifted wanting to tell the world I had now got Jesus in my heart. Of course, at that age, I had not realized then what life was to confront me with, but looking back now from that day on the Lord remained with me seeing me through so many difficulties but never, to this day, letting me go.

Low I Stand At the Door And Knock

As time marches on and our hurrying feet,
Are we rushing on downward through life's busy street,
Are we missing the sound of his constant repeat,
As Jesus knocks on?

As time marches on, can you not hear His call?
Ring through the hovels and grand palace halls,
Through kingdoms may rise, and kingdoms may fall,
Still Jesus knocks on.

Though time marches on, He is still here today,
Stop now and listen, don't turn Him away,
Don't harden your heart or keep Him at bay,
As Jesus knock on.

Yes, time marches on while it's steadily flight,
It is speedily turning the day into night,
Open the door; turn your darkness to light
As Jesus knocks on.

Time marches on, it will all end some day,
Time on this earth will all pass away,
And then at the end forever and aye,
Then comes eternity, what will you say?

Eternity comes and time is no more,
What joy for each heart
That opened the door,
But those who ne'er opened then hell is in store
Eternity friend is forever and more.

Now, think for a while where are you to spend
That dateless, that timeless, that age without end,
Oh, listen and open your heart's door dear friend,
While Jesus knocks on.

MERCY AND GRACE

*Mercy and grace through Christ Jesus
were displayed when He died on the tree,
bringing me into God's favour,
oh, what love He bestowed upon me.*

Mercy And Grace

God' mercy and grace through Christ Jesus,
Broke forth when He died on the cross
And swept ore the hills of transgression,
Seeking the guilty and lost.

When he cried from the cross "It is finished"
Salvation released like a flood,
Torn asunder the vail in the temple,
Giving us access to God.

Yes mercy and grace for the sinner,
Poured out from God's throne from above,
To cover the debt of the guilty,
To forgive with unlimited love.

In torrents it covers the mountains,
Of all our presumptuous sins,
It is free, it is pure, it is priceless,
Sinner for you flooding in,

It flows into unlikely places
Enters hearts prepared to receive,
Streaming in like a mighty ocean,
To the sinner prepared to believe.

God's mercy and grace so abundant,
Amazing, tremendous and free,
You ask me how I receive it,
Repent toward God is the key.

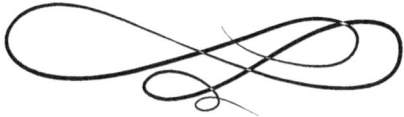

HIS HUMILITY

*See here the humility of Jesus, never
a thought for himself but reaching
out to others. What an example for all
of us to follow.*

His Humility

The humility of Jesus drew me to Him,
The way He lived and walked among the poor,
Taking up the cause of the afflicted
By pharisees and teachers of the law.

Seeking out the humble, poor and homeless,
And sinners like the women at the well,
Deprived, oppressed and lonely people
Would have a story of his love to tell.

Read how He healed the blind man by the road side,
Read how He touched the leper in despair,
And those that cried to Him for mercy,
To seek his touch the Saviour would be there.

The blind man by the road side, He would tell you
How Jesus turned acknowledging his cry,
How many times he'd called for help from others,
But Jesus heard and did not pass him by.

The woman with the blood disease, remember?
While crowds were gathered round, she touched his skirt,
He turned because He knew that she had touched him,
He knew her need and gently healed her hurt.

Those days have gone but Jesus has not altered,
He's still the same today as He was then,
He has not altered since He went to heaven,
His arms of love are still held out to men.

Though He's in heaven now you still can call Him,
In fact, He could be waiting for your call,
He is there when no one else will listen,
There's nothing you can't say, He'll hear it all.

That's because He sees and really knows you,
He knows your thoughts and troubled heart as well,
For no one knows you better than the Saviour,
And you can tell Him all there is to tell.

Though unseen He heals the broken hearted,
And fills the void we often feel in life,
With joy and peace beyond our understanding,
That takes the place of conflict, pain and strife.

Can I suggest you cannot live without Him?
Once you have tried and tested for yourself
The love that died to save us all as sinners
Will fill your life with peace and all its wealth.

This life on earth goes on to what's beyond it,
And Jesus Christ will take you all the way,
When man's small span of life is ended,
Your life goes on to heaven, Oh glorious day.

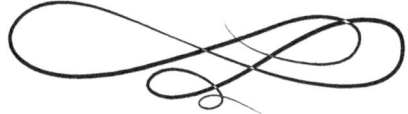

JUST A KISS

*A man came up and the man who was
called Judas, as one of the twelve, was
leading them. He approached Jesus to kiss Him but Jesus asked him
"Judas, are you betraying the Son of
Man with a kiss?"*

Just A Kiss

Just a kiss, it was just a kiss,
Jesus betrayed with just a kiss,
Judas known as a friend of his,
Betrays his Lord with just a kiss.

A treacherous kiss, a deceptive kiss,
By one who professed to have loved Him,
A betraying kiss, such a hurtful kiss,
Increasing the Saviour's sufferings.

For he'd walked with Him,
And he'd talked with Him,
He had sat and eaten his bread with Him,
Such times of bliss but in spite of this,
He betrayed the Lord with just a kiss.

Just a kiss, it was just a kiss,
And thirty pieces of silver,
Was that all He was worth?
Was that all He was worth,
His master and teacher and friend on earth

THIS IS MY MOUNTAIN

*Those who trust in the Lord are
like mount Zion which cannot be
shaken but endures forever.
As the mountains surround Jerusalem
so the Lord surrounds his people
forever and ever.
Psalm 125:1:2*

This is My Mountain

On the mountain of Zion I see the sun rise,
While visions of glory are filling my eyes,
This is my mountain while Christ from above,
Holds me entwines me with thoughts of his love,

This is my mountain where praise never ends,
This is my mountain where incense ascends,
This is my mountain, my inherited land,
Given to me by the Father's own hand.

The Lion of Judah on mount Zion stands,
The Alpha, Omega holds stars in his hand,
Clear rivers of waters, sheer fountains of love,
Enraptures my heart as they flow from above.

See gazelles leaping, they skip with delight,
While fragrant lilies are clothed in pure white,
I lay in green pastures; I'm fed by the hand,
Of the Mighty Omnipotent King of the land.

THOUGHTS OF PARADISE
&
PARADISE WITH ME

*In my Father's house there are many rooms,
if it were not true I would have told you. I am
going there to prepare a place for you. And
If I go and prepare a place for you, I will come
back and take you to be with me that you may
also be where I am. You know the way to the
place where I am going. John 14:1-4*

Thoughts of Paradise

Within God's written Word I see,
A place that He's prepared for me,
I often wonder how it'll be,
And of my loved ones I shall see,
Who the first that I shall meet,
And with what rapture we shall greet.

I have such dreams where it will be,
This place that God's prepared for me,
I gaze into the starry sky,
Is paradise up there in high?
And somewhere in our milky way,
Will be my world some other day?

A world that lies beyond the sun,
We go when earthly days are done,
When pain and weeping are no more,
No cries of anguish, shouts of war,
Where only love and peace exist,
Will paradise be just like this?

No more making wrong decisions,
No more state or church divisions,
No more thieves to brake and enter,
No politician takes the centre,
'Cause Christ my Lord rules over all,
And at his feet in love I'll fall.

It will be my joy to stand with Him,
With hosts of heaven his praise to sing,
And Oh to gaze upon his face,
Who bought me to this very place
To live in his eternal bliss,
My paradise will be like this.

Paradise With Me

The dying thief Christ said would be,
This day in paradise 'with me',
Those words 'with me' my soul suffice,
To be with Him in paradise.

I know that there my soul is free,
To gaze on Christ eternally,
My longing eyes shall see his face,
His glory and his love embrace.

I'll see his hands and pierced side,
The Lamb once slain, now glorified,
In Christ alone my heart delights,
My joy will reach its highest heights.

Tremendous singing will be heard,
And Christ will be in every word,
His sacrifice, his deeds, his love
Resound around those courts above.

Christ said, "In paradise with me"
When life is done that's where I'll be,
"With me" those words my soul suffice,
To be with Him in paradise.

FREE FORGIVENESS
*(The following verses can be sung to
The tune of Londonderry Air)*

*A God so great beyond my apprehension,
A Holy God that cannot look on sin,
Bent down so low and offered free forgiveness,
What love, such love through Christ
My sinful heart to win.*

Free Forgiveness
(Can be sung to the tune of Londonderry Air)

Oh but for Christ who died for me on Calvary,
I'd stand condemned before a righteous God,
The God who sees, the God who is all knowing,
Has marked my ways and seen the path I've trod.
A God so great beyond my apprehension
A Holy God that could not look on sin,
Bent down so low and offered free forgiveness,
His love, such love through Christ my heart to win.

There'll be a day when God will stand in judgment,
And but for Christ, his wrath would fall on me,
For I have heard his anger in the thunder,
And power as in the mighty roaring sea.
His governmental hand, one day will deal with sin,
And yet that God supreme in power and majesty,
Bent down so low and offered free forgiveness,
What love, He has through Christ bestowed on me.

Oh but for Christ when God goes forth in judgment,
Where would I stand? I tremble as I see,
My never dying soul, its destination,
Would be to spend in hell's eternity,
Banished by God, Creator of the earth and sky,
But yet this mighty God enthroned on high,
Bent down so low and offered free forgiveness
And I shall never understand the reason why.

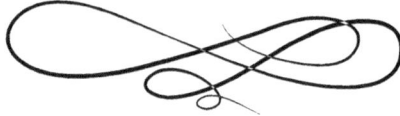

ISAIAH 53

*Just a few impressions I received
after reading Psalm 53. One being how,
"He took my infirmities, carried my sorrow,
with assurance today and bright hope for
tomorrow."*

Isaiah 53

It was as I was reading Isaiah 53
That I learnt of a man that was wounded for me,
Who was smitten, afflicted and pierced for my sin,
And I read all my punishment God laid on Him.

When oppressed and afflicted, He spoke not a word,
Like a sheep before shearers, no sound to be heard,
By oppression and judgment they took Him away,
To bear my transgressions, God struck Him that day.

No violence He did, no deceit in his mouth,
I asked as I read it. "Who is this about?"
I turned to the gospels and there I could see,
To bear my transgressions He hung on a tree.

They pierced Him and mocked Him, afflicted, oppressed,
As an offering for sin He fulfilled God's request,
And now by such grace I'm forgiven and free,
Just as I read in Isaiah 53.

He took my infirmities, carried my sorrow,
With assurance today and bright hope for tomorrow.

PASSING BY

I was looking around an old church in Devon noted for its art work. It was a very hot day and, after a while, I decided to sit down on one of the pews. As I watched the people milling around looking at the art work I noticed a woman looking up at a painting. She had tears in her eyes so I got up and stood beside her to see what was affecting her so deeply.
It was a painting of the crucifixion of Jesus, betrayed with such cruelty, hatred and suffering at the hands of men that it took me some time to take it all in.
After a time the women whispered "You know that's my Saviour". "He's mine as well" I replied. Although we had never met before we were bound with our love for Christ.
I looked around, was there no one else being affected by this painting? It reminded me of the Scripture in Lamentation 1:12. "Is it nothing to you all you who pass by."
As a result of that day, I wrote the following verses.

Passing By

Passing by a church one day, I chose to go inside,
Just to view the art work and other things beside,
The church was full of people surveying such as I,
I sat down on a seat awhile and watched them passing by.

It was then I noticed hanging a painting on the wall,
A painting of the crucifix, in detail I recall,
Such feeling in the art work, "Magnificent thought I,"
While others, unaffected, were simply passing by.

A woman stood beside it, in silence and in awe,
Had she discovered something she had not seen before?
Then as I watched I noticed a tear fall from her eye,
While others, unaffected, were simply passing by.

I made my way towards her and placed my hand in hers,
"He's mine as well" I said "I guess He must be yours."
And so we both stood gazing at that picture lifted high
While others, unaffected, were simply passing by,

High on a cross they'd nailed Him, I remember even now,
The blood from cruel thorns seen running down his brow,
His face portrayed such sadness; I felt I too could cry,
While others, unaffected, were simply passing by.

I saw his torn hands bleeding, those hands that cared and healed,
And stripes upon his shoulders, what hate that scene revealed,
For love they showed Him malice, I whispered softly, "Why"
While others, unaffected, were simply passing by.

I saw such outward torment in that picture on the wall,
It stirred my soul within me and yet that was not all,
God poured his wrath on Jesus, not seen with human eye,
While others, unaffected, were simply passing by.

No human eye could stand it, no human heart conceive,
The wrath of God for sin as Saviour He received,
For then the sun was blackened out, no light could penetrate,
I know not how He suffered then, no painting could relate.

But Oh amid his sacrifice my Lord was heard to cry,
"Eloi, Eloi, lama sabachthani?"

Have you stopped to look at Jesus? See Him there upon the cross,
His arms outstretched to save you; such love to meet man's loss
Have you stopped to look at Jesus? Has a tear rolled down your eye?
Or are you like the others and simply passing by.

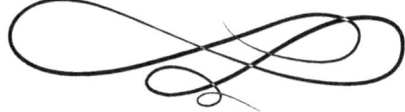

THE EMPTY TOMB

Now Mary stood outside the tomb crying, as she wept she bent over to look into the the tomb and saw two angels in white, seated where Jesus body had been, one at the head the other at the foot, they asked her "Women why are you crying?
"They have taken my Lord away," she said "and I know not where they have put him"
At this she turned round and saw Jesus standing there but she did not realise that it was Jesus.
He asked her," Women why are you Crying? Who is it you are looking for?"
Thinking he was the gardener, she said, "Sir if you have carried him away, tell me where you have put him, and I will get him."
Jesus said to her "Mary". She turned toward him and cried out "Teacher."

The Empty Tomb

While early morning mist yet lay,
To look for Him she went her way,
To find the tomb that marked the spot,
Where Jesus lay in death,
Her Lord had died, there was no sun
Could light her heart, her Lord had gone,
She loved Him such a lot.

Her tears flowed out as in despair,
She reached the tomb, He was not there,
Two angels marked the spot,
He was gone; was lost to sight,
Her life had lost its joy and light,
She loved Him such a lot.

She loved Him as the one whom here
Had met her need and calmed her fear,
But now her Lord was not,
Oh, who had taken Him away?
Please tell her where his body lay,
She loves Him such a lot.

The empty tomb so filled her eye,
That when her living Lord drew nigh,
T'was Him and knew it not,
"O Mary, Mary" Jesus said,
Behold, I've risen from the dead,
I loved you such a lot.

She hears his voice, its sweetest tones,
Rings through her heart, she sees and owns
Her Lord, "but touch me not,
But Mary you must run and tell,
My loved ones I'm alive and well,
I love them such a lot".

Raised from the dead, by God acclaimed,
He lives in heaven, the greatest named,
It's Jesus and He's not ashamed,
Of us no matter what,
We're still his loved ones owned by Him,
Who died to wash away our sin
And loves us such a lot.

BECAUSE CHRIST LIVES

Hearts that were empty; hearts that were broken
Hearts that were heavy and burdened with sin,
Because Christ now lives, because He is risen,
We live again rejoicing in Him.

Because Christ Lives
Can be sung to the tune "Morning has broken"

See the sun set on calvary's hill side,
Evening has come and Jesus has died,
Ending a day of anguish and sorrow,
Leaving his loved ones broken inside.

Hearts that were empty; hearts that were broken,
Hearts full of sorrow, hearts full of gloom,
Lovingly took down the body of Jesus,
Wrapped it in myrrh and laid in a tomb.

See now the stone is rolled from the entrance,
Empty the tomb where Jesus had lain,
Christ is seen risen, Christ is seen living,
Hearts that were broken healed once again.

Hearts that are empty; hearts that are broken,
Hearts that were heavy and burdened with sin,
Because Christ now lives, because He has risen,
We live again rejoicing in Him.

AS A CHILD IN THE LONDON BLITZ

One of my grandchildren asked if I would help her with an essay for school on the London blitz knowing that I, as a child, had been involved when our house had a direct hit losing everything we owned.

As A Child In the London Blitz

As a child, I remember it well,
Relating such stories are still hard to tell,
But grandchildren clamber, "Gran tell us please do,
Those frightening days of World War Two".

Well, surviving those days in the London Blitz,
Like moles underground we tried to exist,
In dim lighted bunkers where nobody calls,
Damp smells up our nostrils, white breeze blocks for walls.

Bunk beds on stations seen lining the walls,
Out of reach from the blast as the doodle-bug falls,
Ambulances, stretchers, folk carried away,
Schools, king, country and parliament pray.

The harsh sound of sirens, the drone of each plane,
The animals howling as if they're in pain,
The searchlights, and plane fights and rubble that lay,
Smouldering still burning by night and by day.

Remembering the day when the morning we woke,
To learn that our home was now rubble and smoke,
All that we owned disappeared over night,
Thank God for those breeze blocks and walls painted white.

No home and no dwelling we're now refugees,
"You don't belong here, go home if you please",
Most refugees would be treated the same,
I can tell you, our childhood was never a game.

When at school in assembly we'd sit up and listen,
When registered called we would see who was missing,
Plane fights called 'dog fights' up there in the sky,
Child, thank the Lord that those days have gone by.

And here in your world, in your world today,
Don't take it for granted just look up and pray,
For who knows the future it's all in God's hand,
He's a purpose in all that we don't understand.

Christmas In the Forties

Christmas in the forties, when the Jerrie's were about
And ration books were needed when food was running out,
There were coupons for our groceries, coupons for our sweets
Coupons for our clothing our furniture and sheets.

Like the good old English we stood through fire and grit,
Though Hitler had begun it all, by gum we finish it,
We kept the home fires burning, the home guard fighting fit,
Standing at the ready and prepared to do our bit.

When the waters boiling and nothing in the pan.
No rations left to fill it we resort to bread spam.
And when the planes were flying with Nazis over head
We'd dive down to the shelter and lay upon our bed.

Sons and fathers absent, and mothers left behind
We deemed to make the Christmas our children had in mind.
With toys and games they long for were not seen in the shops
But we could make a doll's head with paper mash and mops.

The things we couldn't purchase we planned to make our own
Searching through the rubbish tips for things that folk had thrown
For mothers with their children would not see them without
They'd spent their evenings, making presents out of knout.

Said Mrs. Brown, "I've made a doll to meet my child's request
And to this day she never knew it came from dad's old vest."
Said Mrs. Smith, "my child's desire I'll meet because it matters,
With my paint brush and my paint, I'll make her snakes and ladders."

Said Mrs. Todd, "I have three kids and one of them a daughter
I'll give them paper chains to make to stick with flour and water."
Said Mrs. Fox, "there's six of ours that need their stockings filling,
Six bracelets made from silver foil have cost me just a shilling."

Said Mrs. Barns, "for every sock I've made my kids a cracker,
And should I have some money left, I'll buy me Hub. tobacco
And now the kids are sorted out, let's think of Christmas dinner
Open up the ration books and make this year a winner."

Now there's that there turkey I had fattened in the yard?
I had so learnt to love him that I dined on bread and lard
I made a Christmas pudding with brandy nuts and fruit
And afraid it might be stolen so I hid in the boot.

And when the war was over, and the fighting was all done,
We had a great big party, to celebrate we'd won.
We eat doughnuts by the dozens, ham and egg and cheese,
Butter chips and bacon till we were down upon our knees.

When we were down to earth again we said, "Do you suppose
Will generations thank us for the way we stood, who knows?"
But these were mighty women that scraped and scraped to save,
In the days when things were rationed, and our men folk faced the grave.

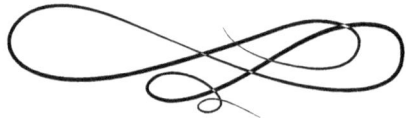

THE PHARISEE

*Having experienced the hardness
cruelty and legality of the law keepers
what a contrast is seen in the Good
Shepherd who searched all night for
the lost sheep laying it on his shoulders
bringing it home rejoicing.*

The Pharisee

As Jesus walked upon this earth, his love an open door,
Drawing sinners to Himself, dispensing mercies store,
The teachers and the pharisees looked on with great disdain,
"This man He welcomes sinners" you could hear them all complain,
"He even eats his bread with them and walks among the poor,
Prophesying to be God, but sets aside the law.

O pharisees O Pharisees, you, teachers of the law,
Full of self-importance, think nothing of the poor,
Lay burdens on the people too heavy to be born,
Fleece them in the temple and look on them in scorn,
You have no time for sinner but to judge them and condemn,
Your harsh and cruel manner adds misery to men.

Now contrast that with Jesus you took and crucified,
The One that you condemned to death with fabricated lies,
If only you would learn from Him the secrets of God's love,
You would see your shameful attitude exposed by God above,
Now come and see this picture in the story Jesus told,
Of one sheep from a hundred who had wandered from the fold.

Imagine in the mountain you have sadly lost you way,
In the hills at night time where adverse dangers lay,
Lost and cold and terrified, how will you spend the night?
You tremble in the darkness a cold and lonely sight,
You say "From out of ninety nine will He be missing me?
Would He bother in a night like this to come and rescue me?"

For who would walk these mountains to search for one lost sheep,
When knowing back at home He still had ninety-nine to keep,
Who would wonder hill and dale until He found the lost,
Searching till He finds you, are you really worth the cost?
You, hard and loveless pharisees I dare you to confess,
You'd leave the sheep on mountain tops to die in their distress.

But Jesus, the good Shepherd, surpassing what you thought,
Will search until he finds it and home rejoicing bought,
O pharisee, O pharisee, what else is there to say,
Take a look at Jesus and handle souls his way.

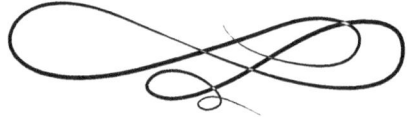

EDEN

*This world we live in is not the world God
Intended it to be, Satan was there at the
Very beginning of the creation ready to destroy
The Eden God had created.
But God is not thwarted; there is a new
Eden awaiting his redeemed.*

Eden

How fair the earth when time began,
And God in Eden made a man,
How blessed among the trees he walked,
And daily with his Maker talked.

Tranquil, happy with delight,
Was man's beginning pure and bright,
Such joy and happiness surpassed,
'Till Satan's evil eye was cast,
Surveyed the scene, "This shall not last",
And slid into a serpents mask.

So Eden's garden treed and grassed
Destroyed by Satan very fast,
He took the rains, the garden's gone,
There's evil now where beauty shone,
Around the earth in sad refrain,
Are fears of war and shouts of pain.

From ever darkening skies arise,
The orphans and the widows cries
Open graves, a slaughtered race,
And refugees that have no place,
Children battered used for sport,
Thousands unborn babies abort.

Broken homes and battered wives,
See how the homeless live their lives,
Satan gloats, he stands elated,
Spoilt the world that God created,
Eden's days for ever gone,
Where love and righteousness once shone.

God saw the creature He had made,
And in compassion came to save,
He saw the lives of men distraught,
And to this world salvation bought,
He wrote a plan, men souls to win,
Through Jesus Christ to cancel sin.

Good news for men the whole world through,
To change your life and make things new,
He seeks the lost, the lame, the blind,
Healing scars sin leaves behind,
He'll free you from your load of sin,
And heaven's gates you'll enter in.

There Eden's garden far and bright,
Now seen in heaven for your delight.
It's gone from earth, sin made it so,
It's gone where Satan cannot go,
Where weeds and brambles cannot spoil,
And those in Jesus Christ are loyal.

Eden's yours if you believe
And Jesus as your Lord receive.

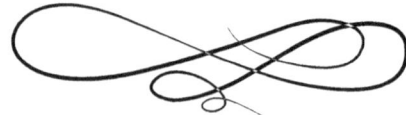

SPEAKING OF KINGS

A King despite a crown of thorns
No ruby crown his head adorns,
No earthly recognition seeks,
Or in self-defense He speaks,
But bending low He bends his head,
As to a wooden cross He's led.

Speaking of Kings

When we speak of a king you know what we mean,
He's powerful, he's rich and we bow when he's seen,
His birth in a palace is heralded by all,
But born in a stable that won't do at all.

When we speak of a king you know what we mean,
He lives a grand life clothed in garments serene,
His servants around him all answer his call,
But live as a carpenter won't do at all.

When we speak of a king you know what we mean,
When he dies he is buried, such splendour is seen,
He is paraded through streets and honoured by all,
But die on a cross, that won't do at all.

When we think of a king you know what we mean,
He's powerful and rich, while his wife is made queen,
He has power in his hand to demand and to call,
But lowly and humble that won't do at all.

When we speak of a king you know what we mean,
A crown set with rubies while emeralds shine green,
As he sits on his throne in a kings' regal hall
But a crown made of thorns, that won't do at all.

When we talk of a king you know what we mean,
He wears on his fingers by all to be seen,
Rings set with diamonds at his grand palace ball
But nails through his hands, no that won't do at all.

I've heard of a king and his subjects I've seen,
They tell how He loves them and washes them clean,
And there in green pastures they rest as He feeds them,
Giving them life and unlimited freedom.

Dissolving their troubles, dispelling their fears,
Soothing their sorrows and drying their tears,
And for their wrong doings He died in their stead,
Nails through his hands and thorns for his head.

Beatings and scourging so humbly He bore,
To keep and to hold us, what king could do more?

WAS IT BY CHANCE

*How many intelligent people have insisted
that God does not exist?
I might not be as bright as some, but I can't
see you can create something out of nothing.
with no one there to create something out
of nothing.*

Was It By Chance

At collage they taught me God didn't exist,
And without much thought I accepted all this,
They said life's beginnings were only by chance,
Through millions of years we slowly advanced,
From monkeys to cavemen then humans they say,
And now we're the people that we are today.

But now that I'm older and wiser I feel,
I study creation and study what's real,
Is it by chance that I'm living today?
In a world oh so intricate, what can I say?
Was it by chance over so many years?
That we are alone with no God that hears?

Is there no one to know if I'm good or I'm bad?
And no one to care if I'm happy or sad?
Is it by chance that this heart in my chest
That no one commands but it beats without rest?
Is it by chance from my toes to my face?
Every joint, every sinew is in the right place?

Is it by chance that my kidneys and liver,
My lungs and my spleen all faithfully deliver?
Now as I'm passing I mention in brief
Is it by chance we get two sets of teeth?
Is it by chance that I wake and I sleep?
And by chance I've emotions to laugh and to weep?

Is it by chance there is hair in my nostrils,
That gathers the dust that could damage my tonsils?
Is it by chance I have wax in my ears,
That wards off the insects that might have ideas?
Is it by chance when I plant that I find,
Every seed that I plant it grows up its own kind?

Is it by chance that all natures bright scenes,
Are softened in beauty by right shades of greens?
Is it by chance there is salt in the sea?
With all those dead bodies, how putrid t'would be,
Is it by chance that the sea draws sea water?
From the oceans in clouds to disperse where it oughter?

Bringing fresh water from sea to the land,
Without any salt and without any sand,
See this is a problem I can't understand,
That this all comes about with no Maker at hand,
Is it by chance that the earth has four seasons?
The farmer will tell you there are four for good reasons.

Or is there a chance that it wasn't by chance
And there is a Creator who planned in advance?
Is it by chance that a world that is round?
That no one falls off or is flung to the ground?
Is it by chance that the sun in the sky,
Is never too close and is never too high?

Who holds the sun and the moon in their place,
If no one is holding them up there in space?
Is it by chance we have males and females,
With productive organs and all that entails?
They tell me no reason has ever been found,
To prove a creator was ever around.

So how did the universe come into being?
How did they exist, all those things we are seeing?
I ponder by day and I reason by night,
These things that you tell me, how can they be right?
Although I'm quite simple less learned than they,
But I still have the right to prove what they say.

Am I in a universe, who knows how large,
Spinning around with no one in charge?
With no one controlling or holding in place
Each star in its orbit that circles in space?
It's frightening to think that no one single soul,
Watches or guides them or keeps them controlled.

Or is it by chance that these things I have mentioned,
Were all bought about by the makers invention?
That someone up there gave the universe birth,
A God who designed and prepared life on earth?
Then said the Creator, "Come let us make man"
And that is precisely how life here began.

God created the world by the word of his mouth,
From the dawn of creation our God was about,
The Lord of the heavens He did it his way,
And into man's souls built his own D and A,
At Collage they told me God didn't exist,
But I'm no longer fooled as I don't believe this.

ONE DENOMINATION

*When I first left my old church, which
had taught me from childhood that ours
was the only true church, I found it
difficult amid all the different ways that
other churches gathered to worship
to find a church that met my needs
at the time. Yes, I found one, but it made
me realize this:
That out of all the confusion there is in
Christendom the Lord knows those that
are truly his.*

One Denomination

They from different congregations,
Represent denominations,
With their rules and regulations,
Holding fast their doctrinations,
Pass them on to their relations,
Live their lives by demonstrations,
Preaching, hailing exaltations,
Circulars and preparations.

Waking men to realisation,
God holds the key to their salvation,
Loud and long their exclamations,
Theirs is the right denomination,
Just think of all the devastation,
If one suggests amalgamation,
Each church combines their doctrinarians.

Think of all the hesitations,
Long and thoughtful conversations,
Leaders gathering informations
Debates and long drawn considerations,
Documents and presentations,
Arguments and declarations
Firm and heated acclamations,
Holding fast their sects foundations.

Each affirm by revelation,
Their's the right denomination,
Words to prove their doctrinatians,
Principals and violations,
My view through simple observations,
To merge would bring too much frustration
Arguments and declarations,
Why break our current good relations?

Christ showed us all by demonstration,
His love, his cross, his declaration,
One church secured by his salvation,
In heaven just one huge congregation,
In heaven there'll be no complications,
In heaven no denominations,
Restrictions, and no regulations,
These will all have passed away,
And only those in Christ will stay.

JOSEPH

*I would love to know more of
Joseph as Scripture has only given us
a few facts. He must have been a man
who had earned Gods trust and respect
as we see him fulfilling his role as the father
so commendably.*

Joseph

"Now in your Christmas story you proclaim each Christmas day,
No one ever seems to ask what I may have to say,
Those privileged days I spent with Him are precious to my heart,
So let me have a chance to tell just how I played my part.

"I, Joseph, took the father's role and watched this baby grow,
Held secrets of his childhood days that others would not know,
For I was not a writer like Matthew, Luke and John,
So records of his younger days have unrecorded gone.

"I was just a carpenter, who lived a humble life,
Yet God entrusted Jesus to me and to my wife,
He helped me in the work place and there He learnt my trade,
And showed such great perfection in everything He made.

"We took Him to the temple when He was only twelve,
We lost Him, when we found Him He was not by Himself,
He was sitting in the temple, sharing with his peers,
Listening, asking questions, beyond his tender years.

"We knew that He was special when angels came to earth,
To tell us that his coming would be by virgin birth,
I know I had the privilege to watch that baby grow,
But yours the greatest honour for you can get to know.

"This Jesus as your Saviour and claim Him as your own,
Your Bible has revealed it, yes; God has made it known,
That though they crucified Him God raised Him from the grave
And now He lives in heaven his arms outstretched to save."

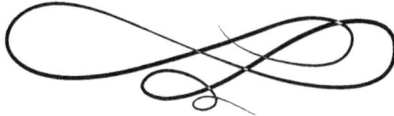

CHRISTMAS POEMS

*The following eight poems are snip-its
from Christmas productions we did
with the youth groups and performed
before the congregation. I felt slipping a
poem or two in can add more feeling to the message.*

No Room

"No room", cried the innkeeper long, long ago,
"No room", they all cried, "we don't want to know,"
"No room", cried the man, who is merry with wine,
"No room", cried the house wife, "we haven't the time"

"No room" cried the children with parcels untied
That need to be opened to see what's inside.
"No room", said the tradesman afraid, "I must dash,
With Christmas upon us I must take the cash."

"No room" cried the cook, "so much shopping to do,"
And the postman's excuse, he's got cards to push through,
It's Christmas remembered? When Christ came to earth,
And yet you've no time to remember his birth.

"I've room", said the baby, "this stable of mine,Is open to any, who stop and find time,"
"I've time" said the child in the temple at twelve,
"To teach you the Scriptures concerning myself."

"I've time", said the Saviour to wash all your feet,
To heal and to comfort poor souls that I meet.

"The lame and the blind and the widow of Nain,
The heartaches and sorrows that cause you such pain.

"There was room in my heart when I died on the tree,
Is there room in your heart this Christmas for me?"

The Truth of Christmas

Let's explain the truth of Christmas,
How profits from of old,
With such perfect accuracy,
The birth of Christ foretold,
We have heard how the disciples
Saw prophecies fulfilled,
Relating to Christ's birth and life,
And how men had Him killed.

It has proved no fancy story,
That's repeated every year,
To add to Christmas festivals,
And traditions as it were,
No it definitely happened,
Near two thousand years ago,
The Son of man came down to earth,
That we his love might know

So every time the stories told,
Remember it's all true,
And the reason for his coming,
Was the work He had to do
By hanging on a shameful cross,
He bore God's judgment rod,
To free man from their sinful past,
And bring us back to God.

Where is He?

Where is He, that lay within a manger?
In swaddling clothes and laying in a bed of straw?
Our selfish occupation missed the Lord of glory,
No room we've cried and left Him with the poor.

Where is He, who slept among the cattle?
A lonely outcast proved by humble birth.
We slept and did not hear the angels story,
That God had come from heaven to dwell on earth.

Pray where is He that I gave no reception?
No room, no place where He could lay his head?
Oh, we despised and counted Him as worthless,
But humble shepherds sort Him out instead.

Where is He born in such bleak conditions?
Amid such cold and hardness on my part?
Oh, that I could find Him like those shepherds,
To bring some gift to cheer and warm his heart.

Where is He for whom my heart is seeking?
I see around me hopelessness and loss,
Pray where is He, whose birth I'm celebrating?
"My friend, they took and hung Him on a cross."

And at that cross is where I found the Saviour
And at that cross is where you'll find Him too,
His journey only started at the stable
And ended with his life laid down for you.

Start your journey to the stable and the manger,
Trace his three and thirty years He spent on earth,
Trace his life, his death and then his resurrection,
And join with us to celebrate his birth.

The Gift

Come see the gift our God bestows,
Upon our human race,
Unwrap the swaddling clothes, behold,
The blessed Saviour's face,
A gift above all other gifts,
Its price? Oh, who can tell?
This priceless gift is only known,
By those redeemed from hell.

Have you embraced this priceless gift?
Or does it worthless lay,
Abandoned on the stable floor,
Still lying in the hay?
O reader if you knew its worth,
If we could only tell,
How much this gift has meant to us,
It could be yours as well.

O God we thank you for your gift,
We worship and adore,
Greater love you could not give,
Or could have given more,
Jesus Christ your only Son,
Sent down from heaven to earth,
No wonder myriad angels sang,
When heralding his birth.

Giving praise to God on High,
And peace to men on earth.

The Census

Now a census is called from God's kingdom above,
For a place in his city, ruled only by love,
It's a land that is perfect, no trouble or strife,
But your name must be down in the "Lamb's Book of Life".

A census is called, is your name in that book?
Have you answered the call? Stop and think, take a look,
When its pages are opened, will your name be there?
Will you with Christ Jesus eternity share?
When the census is finished and all is laid bare,
I wonder, my friend, will your name be in there?

The World's Creator Comes to Earth

The mighty one of untold worth,
The world's Creator comes to earth,
Not in grandeur, robes and splendour,
But lowly as an infant tender.

Not in the place where nobles centre,
But in a shed where all my enter,
From the lowest to the greatest,
Rich or poor what ere their status.

You only have to bow your head,
To find Him in a cattle shed,
Come enter in and apprehend,
Jesus Christ, the sinner's friend.

The Heavenly Story

You've heard the heavenly story,
How God came down to earth,
A lonely, homeless stranger,
Few cared to know his worth.

He felt the hurt of loneliness,
And pain of earths rejection,
Just a few wise men and shepherds,
Where there at his reception.

See shepherds stood in wonder,
At the amazing sight,
For God of all creation,
Had come to earth that night.

And wise men came to worship,
The King of heaven and earth,
They understood his greatness,
In the light of virgin birth.

Shepherd's Speak

"I see this child, I take his hand,
A hand so small and frail,
They'll take this hand again someday,
And pierce with iron nail.

"I bow and stroke his tender brow,
A babe so newly born,
Some day his little head will bear
The marks of cruel thorn.

"And see I hold his tinny feet,
That later on will tread,
A road uphill to calvary,
His precious blood to shed."

Wise Men

Now wise men came to worship,
The King of heaven and earth,
Who understood his greatness
In spite of human birth.

A crown of thorn, a bag of nails,
A wooden cross, a hammer,
By sacrifice this child will die,
By harsh and cruel manner.

A mocking crowd, while judgment falls,
He bears the wroth of sin,
The sins of all who ever ask,
A free forgiveness given.

For us that cannot save ourselves,
Our God provides a way,
This babe will grow to be a man,
And take our sins away.

The heavens sang *"hosanna"*,
And myriad angels sang,
Rejoice for man's salvation,
This night has just begun.

The Christmas Story

Have you heard the Christmas story?
How God came down in love?
The Maker of the universe,
And all the stars above
How He left the heavenly splendour,
So He could let men know,
The nature of his caring heart,
And how He loved them so.

You have your tinsel round the walls,
Crackers, cards and laughter,
In festive mood, but can I ask
Is this really what God's after?
Amid the lights of Christmas trees,
A still small voice calls you,
Don't let the years go rolling by,
But this year think it through.

Why did the Saviour come to earth,
In such a lowly way?
Why do we celebrate his birth
Each year on Christmas day?
Read the gospel Luke wrote,
And watch it all unfold,
The wonders of the virgin birth,
In the account he told.

It's not some fancy story,
Repeated every year,
To add to Christmas festives,
And traditions as it were,
No, it definitely happened,
Near two thousand years ago,
The Son of God came down to earth,
Because He loved us so.

As once again the story's told,
Remember it's all true,
That when He came from heaven above,
He had his eye on you,
And all those years He's waited,
For you to seek Him out,
And truly know within your heart
What Christmas is about.

YOUR WAYS ARE NOT MY WAYS

*This was written when our hearts were
breaking at the sudden death of Roy O'Hara,
our daughter Tina's husband, who the Lord took
in his sleep. He left behind two babies,
three- year- old Bradley and three- month-old
Callum.*

Your Ways Are Not My Ways

Your ways are not our ways; help me understand,
For I'm not yet in tune with the things you have planned,
Why take to yourself a father of two,
And leave a young widow dependent on you?
A five-month-old child and a small boy of three,
Your ways are not my ways, Lord, help me to see.

Your wisdom and greatness are far beyond me,
I know I must trust you although I can't see,
In sorrow and sadness, in darkness of death,
When hearts that are breaking and tears take our breath,
Your ways are not my ways, help me understand,
How there is wisdom and love in the things you have planned.

When trees of the fields shed their leaves and lay bare,
Lifeless, forlorn in the cold winter's air,
Yet burst into life by the power of your hand,
Majestically feeding and shielding the land,
Though bare is my heart on these cold winter days,
May it break forth in spring to your worship and praise?

May we rest in your love through these days of despair?
Awaiting the time when the fruit will be there,
When cold winds are biting, the ground hard and bare,
Be patient in knowing you'll always be there,
Like sun melts the frost in the days of the spring,
May we burst from the darkness your praises to sing?

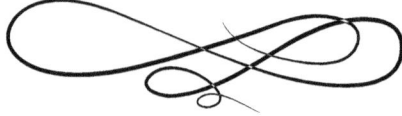

DON'T BE A BLOB

*Written for a young lad who was serving
a custodial sentence.
I wish my young friend could see
what the continual use of drugs
had done to him. Once a bright and
intelligent boy, now behind bars.
The boy he once was had gone, his
brain just a blob.
He knows how many times I have
prayed for him.*

Don't Be A Blob

A blob's just a blob; it is shapeless and baggy,
Can't lift itself up as it's spineless and saggy,
A blob's just a blob; it has no definition,
Slithers along with no aim or ambition.

They enter our homes causing sighs and divisions
Thoughtless and useless at making decisions,
A blob looks for blobs as everyone knows,
A blob makes more blobs wherever it goes.

Blobs slumber all day; then they come out at night,
They drink lots of liquor and blobs like a fight,
They live for the present as if no tomorrow,
He doesn't like work but begging to borrow.

His eyes are distorted, he can't see ahead,
So he could be a blob till the day he is dead,
A blob's for himself; he has no time for others,
His mum or his dad or his sisters and brothers.

Not much conversation; no, not much at all,
When you hear a blob speaking his vocabulary's small,
It's either "I want, give me that, or a grunt",
And sponging on others, he's up there in front.

There are so many blobs all around us today,
Please take my warning and don't go their way,
They are there on street corners behaving like mugs.
Enticing the weak to partake of their drugs.

Joy riding, drinking and burning out cars,
And you'll find very often land up behind bars,
Don't be a blob; get yourself a career,
Or you'll end up a frailer in this life I fear.

Your life is so precious you have only the one,
Don't waste it away until it's all done,
This secret I've learnt and would like to pass on,
I once sort for happiness fervent and long.

All sorts of avenues, pleasures I sort,
Until I discovered what happiness bought,
Thinking for others forgetting yourself,
It's the way to be happy with spiritual wealth.

TRUST IN THE LORD

On July 4, my niece Annie and her husband were told she was carrying Siamese twins that were joined in such a way they could not be separated and, therefore, they would not live. Doctors suggested they had them aborted but after much prayer they decided it was not up to them to terminate life so carried the pregnancy to full term.
The little girls Amber and Chloe were born joined at the chest with just one heart between them, which was outside the rib cage. They lived for four hours then God took them to Himself.

Trust In The Lord

O God the Unsearchable, Ancient of days,
No earthling can fathom or question your ways,
God of the universe, faithful and wise,
Who stooped down to save us and opened our eyes,
The God who just spoke and creation obeys,
Yet we, as your children, still question your ways,
The road you have mapped and the route you have planned
Were written and sealed by the fathers' own hand.

So help us to trust you through life's journey here,
Through sorrow remind us that you're always near,
O God the Unsearchable, Ancient of days,
Uphold your children through hazardous ways,
Oh God of all ages we know you are here,
We call on your presence to comfort and cheer,
And thank you for Samuel, Annie and Paul,
Through pressures these three have reminded us all

In trouble be patient in seeking your face,
Knowing nothing you've ordered will be out of place,
You commanded the wind and the waves to be still,
As you do for all who accept your will,
We saw Annie and Paul preparing to wait,
For the storm to pass and the wind abate,
Never hastening or ending but seeing it through,
Just waiting on God for what they should do.

Not aborting but quietly they weathered the storm,
Till your babies, dear Amber and Choe were born,
O God the Unchangeable, Ancient of days,
No creature can fathom or question your ways,
Though fruitless Annie's labour, or as it all seemed,
Ending long months with an unfulfilled dream,
But God wrote this page in his own hand of love,
Predestined those babies to his own world above.

One heart but two soul He has claimed as his own,
And took them untainted, made heaven their home,
And way back in time before sin became rife,
He wrote those babies' names in the Lamb's book of life,
And now in his arms they are held in his care,
Embraced in his love which one day we'll share,
Not till the end when each chapter is read,
And each page fulfilled in the way that He said.

Will we see the whole picture his love has designed?
To make us the children that He had in mind,
O God, the Unsearchable, Ancient of days,
How wonderful, marvellous are all your ways.

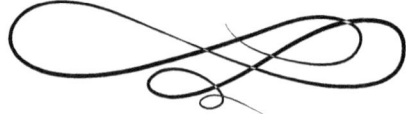

SEEK THE LORD WHILE HE MAY BE FOUND

Are we endlessly searching for the truth?
As I was when I left my old church,
we are told so much and taught so much
but there comes a time when the truth has
to be searched out for ourselves and we
have to be established in what is truth
and untruth. I have to find Christ
for myself.

Seek The Lord While He May Be Found
Call Upon Him While He's Near

I see three travellers coming up the pathway,
Their countenance displays a heavy load,
Tied by a somewhat distant journey,
Weary by a long and distant road.

"What brings you to this church this time of morning?
You look as though you may have lost your way,
Tell us, travellers what may be your business?
We'd like to hear your story if we may."

Travellers

"We seek the one of whom the prophets told us,
He, who Micah prophesied would come,
From Bethlehem to rule among his people,
Whose origins from old, the Ancient One."

Where is this one who heads the Christmas story?
Whom angels sang to celebrate his birth?
And lonely shepherds dazzled by his glory
Heard them sing, 'Good will to men on earth'?

"We searched the hills but everywhere was silent,
No heavenly choir was heard or angels sang,
Though sheep still graced upon the hill side,
The sky was dark the messengers long gone.

We trod the road the shepherds would have taken,
To Bethlehem, the place He entered earth,
The town folk said they'd take us to the stable,
The very place the virgin gave Him birth.

The stable door was swinging off its hinges,
An empty cave was all that met our eyes,
A damp and eerie silence hung around us,
Our echoes sending back a haunting sigh.

The babe has gone, no longer in the stable,
Nothing left that history could supply,
Just the cattle trough where they had laid Him,
The Child's birth, that scene had long gone by.

They even told us Herod may have slain Him,
In the slaughter he demanded of that day,
Purposely to slay the One we're seeking,
This caused our hearts to sink in dark dismay.

Then others told us God Himself preserved Him,
And Herod's plan had simply come to nought,
They assured us one day we might find Him,
To carry on and seek the One we sought."

Church
Now said the church, "you'll find Him in the Scriptures,
In the book that God wrote of Himself,
No need to travel far and wide to find Him,
We've many Bibles here upon our shelf.

"Open up its pages, there you'll see Him,
The very One to whom you long to meet,
And like those shepherds when you've found Him,
With hearts fulfilled you'll worship at his feet."

RELIGIOUS RELIGIONS

I did not find Christ in religion
or in the naming of a church
or in a magnificent church building
I did not find Him in church rules
or in church traditions
or in the garments of a priest.
I found Him in his people, humble
gentle people who gave to me Christ's
love at times I needed most.

Religious Religions

Religious leaders of our day
With different presentations,
Would like us all to join their church
To boost their congregations.
Hear each voice, then take your choice,
For Christian preservation.

If you're a Baptist through and through
You'll know what they expect of you,
One cannot join, you realize,
If you have never been baptized.

Then if you are a Methodist,
It's on good work your church exists
Be kind, be good to one another
Treat all mankind as if your brother.

Now holy brethren stand alone,
The Scriptures and the truth they own,
You cannot join without a hat,
No ifs or buts, cause that is that.

Then C. of E. with prayers and creeds,
All their prayers they have to read,
The vicar turns up in a dress,
With crosses hanging round his chest.

The Pentecostals love their bands,
They dance and sing and raise their hands,
On each Lord's day they stand to pray,
And to their music swing and sway.

But if like me you cannot choose,
Or understand religious views,
You do not have to be a part
As long as Christ is in your heart.

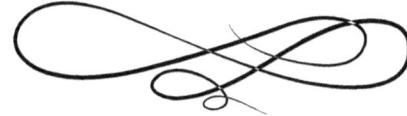

THE MASTER PAINTER

Written for our 40th wedding anniversary.
reflecting as we looked back the joys
and sorrows we had shared together and
God's faithfulness through it all.

The Master Painter

The Master took his canvas on the day that we were wed,
And carefully mixed his colours with blue sky's overhead,
The sun in brightest colours He paints amid the blue,
Then He paused for just a moment for the bride and broom to view.

Blue skies and the sunshine was all there was to see,
The rest an empty canvas for the things that were to be,
Blue skies and sunshine a cloudless new beginning,
Blue skies and sunshine with wedding bells still ringing.

But the artist had not finished; there was more for Him to do,
The honeymoon now over it was time to set the view,
So the Master took his paint brush, in detail paints the scene,
With mountain tops and valleys and fields of varied green.

There came houses, there came churches and children at our feet,
Then lots and lots of people we were privileged to meet,
Precious moments so recorded by the Master painter's hand,
And every scene He painted was exactly as He planned.

See brighter colours merging as the Master paints each scene,
With happy days and laughter in the places we had been,
The pathways we had trodden, the roads that we had run,
With the wonders of our married life since we became as one.

Then there came the shadings that no painter misses out,
Small patches on the grassland, in valleys vast amounts,
That's when He took his water colours, mixed them with our tears,
And told us both to trust Him throughout the coming years.

It is often in those dark times when the shadings going on,
We see dark paint in his palette, is the picture going wrong?
Will it spoil the art work when He dabs it all with gray?
Can we really trust Him while He's painting it this way?

If we paint the picture our way, would it be a big mistake?
And find it's not the picture that the Master wants to paint,
So we put our hands in his hands as He sees us through the pain,
For sure He sees how hard it is to try and paint the rain.

He has visions for our canvas before the world began,
Before He died and rose again when He became a man,
And through the darkest shadows and through the blackest night,
He washed away sins crimson stain to make the canvas white.

Now in those darkest places where the sun cannot be seen,
Where shadows in the valleys have hid the shades of green,
I hear the painter whisper in no uncertain tone,
I will never leave you to paint it on your own.

And faithful to his promise the Painter still paints on,
Painting in the details of all the years that's gone,
He paints a perfect picture with the skill of his own hand,
Can we use it to help to others just as the Master planned?

WHO IS THIS MAN?

This poem was written in memory of my much loved grandson, Luke Moulding who gave himself to the Lord at an early age but after a long illness of depression stood in front of a train ending his life at twenty nine.

Who Is This Man?

Who is this Man that walks upon the waters?
And bids the waves and billows to be still,
Who, by his will creates a vast expansion?
Of sun, moon and stares all subject to his will?
It is the Lord, who understands earth's sorrows,
The Lord who wept when Lazarus had died
Is with us now and understands our sadness,
Who feels with us and stores the tears we've cried.

Who is this Man God likened to a shepherd?
Who searches night and day for one lost sheep?
One child, one son lost in life's stream of madness,
One boy who slipped and could not find his feet,
But Jesus found and placed him on his shoulders,
He found him there upon a railway track,
And took him home, home to himself rejoicing,
From earth to heaven to claim his lost son back.

Who is this Man who gave Himself for sinners?
And took upon Himself the debt we owe?
So those who look to Him may be forgiven,
They ask not who He is because they know,
Our hearts respond in love beyond our sorrow,
Rejoice in Him, who feels our every pain,
We have a hope we have a bright tomorrow,
With Christ and when our loved ones meet again.

Christ broke the chains of sin and death that bind us,
And those that trust in Him will see his face,
Will live forever in the Saviours' presence,
Made perfect through Christ's death; what love, what grace.
To be forever living in his presence,
All earth's painful sorrows turned to bliss,
Rejoicing in a land of milk and honey
His faithful ones absorbing all of this.

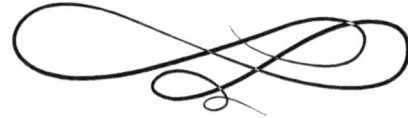

TALES REPEATEDLY TOLD

*I often think how far man would have
advanced if we did not have to go over
the same lessons our grandparents learnt
to be learnt again by the next generation.
We advance with one generating and
start again with the next.*

Tales Repeatedly Told

We are the children the young of today,
And need the experience of old folk they say,
That the youth has its place at the feet of the old,
Listening to stories repeatedly told.

They tell us such tales of their troubles and strife,
Then tell us those days were the best days in life,
In their day they did this, in their day they did that,
Unheard of to answer their mums and dads back.

Their mothers were strict and their fathers were stern,
We must be obedient or we'll never learn,
We know when these stories are going to be told,
Cause they bring out the parchments and smooth out the folds.

When we slip and we slide in the things that we do,
And get into trouble, they say, "We told you".
If you'd listened to us with this and with that,
You probably wouldn't be just where you're at.

But when they were younger and not quite so old,
Did they hearken the things that their grandparents told?
Or spurn what they told them and scoffed their advice,
Then learnt those same stories the hard way in life.

At the end of the day when we're all old and gray,
Will experience tell us what they had to say?
Will we fetch out our parchments and smooth out the folds?
Tell the same stories our grandparents told?

When we visit their graves to replenish their flowers,
Will we find all their stories have now become ours?

POOR ALBERT

I wrote this for our youth group showing how quickly Satan can get in and destroy their young lives (Adapted from Albert and The lion).

Poor Albert

We've a nice little church right here where we live,
Where preaching and teaching are done,
Where Mr. and Mrs. Ramsbottom,
Attended with Albert their son.

Now a bad little lad was young Albert,
You youngsters take heed while I tell,
How he'd sit eating sweets during sermon,
And drop all his litter as well.

Then he'd sit and he'd gaze out of window,
And think "What am I doing here,
When I could have been out in the sunshine,
Playing football or rugby, Oh dear.

"And that feller up there on the platform,
Keeps quoting the Bible but 'Gee',
He might understand what he's saying,
But it don't make no since, not to me.

"One day I may be a Christian,
Live my life like me old mum and dad,
But those blokes I am hanging around with,
Say there is so much more fun to be had.

"So I'm not coming here next Sunday,
But something exciting I'll do,
I'm going to go off in the sunshine,
To spend the whole day at the zoo."

So next week when time for the service,
Young Albert were not to be found,
He'd gone with the lions and the tigers,
For excitement young Albert was bound.

Sure enough at the zoo was young Albert,
Just looking around as you do,
For monkeys and camels and tigers,
And a lion at Whipsnade zoo.

Now Albert had heard about lions,
How they were ferocious and wild,
And to see ugly beast there so peaceful,
Just didn't seem right to the child.

It were more than young Albert could handle,
So he whispered in old Satan's ear,
"Wake up I want some excitement,
I'm fed up and bored near to tears.

For years I've been sitting through sermons,
While what they may say might be right
But obeying your parents and so on,
Such restrictions I feel are too tight."

Now Satan he sat up and listened,
"You're right there young Albert my boy,
You've got to get out on the streets there,
Have fun boy life's there to enjoy."

Now Albert thought Satan was honest,
And he'd found a good friend he could trust,
So he slid himself under the barrier,
Covering his trousers in dust.

"It's a shame" Albert said as he stood there,
"That these barriess are between you and me,
Why do folk put up such restrictions?"
Said Satan, "Do you want the key"?

Said Albert, "You got the key then?"
"Not here, but I know where it is,"
"Then tell me", said Albert, "I'll get it,"
Then "listen", said Satan to this.

"Go down to the pub on the corner,
Find the man with long hair and a fringe,
Smoking crack, selling drugs to teenagers,
And giving away a syringe.

"Get friendly and join in the business,
Offer him whiskey and gin,
By then you'll have got in his favour,
And he'll give you the key to get in.

So while our church was having their service,
Young Albert was out on the job,
While we were all singing Gods praises,
Young Albert was out with the mob.

Now Satan, the lion, grew restless,
Wondering where Albert could be,
But was over the moon when he saw him,
Approaching his cage with the key.

"Good lad" said the lion, "You've done it
"Now hurry son, open the door,
Without all these's bars and restrictions,
We'll get to know each other more."

So in went the key in the keyhole,
And round went the key in the lock,
But as soon as the cage door was open,
Poor Albert was in for a shock.

For old Satan pounced in excitement,
But Albert, Oh Albert poor soul,
Before you could say "Bob's your uncle,"
He'd grabbed him and swallowed him whole.

Poor Albert, too late; he was swallowed,
You young folk you must be aware,
If you take the same road as young Albert,
You too will end up in there.

THE MAN WITH THE LIGHT

*I came home from work one night to
find the house in complete darkness.
I discovered it to be an electric fault and
had to call out an electrician. It was a
couple of hours before he turned up, so
I could do nothing else but peer into the
darkness just longing for the light.*

The Man With The Light

Returning from work to my home one night,
I reached for the switch to turn on the light,
But something was wrong; I was soon made aware,
Though the switch was turned on the light was not there.

"Oh the bulb must have gone" I said to myself,
"There's a new one I know on the kitchen shelf,"
So groping my way through the darkened hall,
I felt for the switch on the kitchen wall.

Now changing the bulb was a small thing to do,
It would only take me a minute or two,
So I stood on a chair, held onto the socket,
Put in the new and the old in my pocket.

With the flick of the switch, should it be nothing worse,
Then the light will go on and the darkness disperse,
But it wasn't the bulb when the switch went on,
I was still in the dark; there was something else wrong.

The power had gone off, could this be a fuse?
Or may be a power cut, I thoughtfully mused,
But the view from my window definitely showed,
The lights were still burning across the road.

Well it can't be a power cut, I began to feel sure,
It must be a fuse; it can't be much more,
The fuse box I knew was above the front door.
But I'd never yet opened a fuse box before.

There were 15 amp 13 amp 5 amp and 3.
There was no one to tell me which one it should be.
By changing it, would I do more harm than good?
So I phoned for a man that I knew understood.

Alone in the dark I sat waiting the time,
To the tick of the clock and occasional chime
It was dark and eerie as long shadows fell,
From the oak tree outside, I remember it well.

Its branches threw shapes that would rise and fall,
As their movements were haunting the kitchen wall,
Nervous and cold now imagining things,
In the dim distortion the darkness brings.

Then at last came the man I knew understood,
And he lit up my life like I knew he would,
For the shadows dispersed as the lights went on,
Fear and the loneliness suddenly gone.

The joy of that moment remains with me still,
That feeling of freedom to move where I will,
The light in the room shone so radiantly bright,
Exchanging my darkness and shadows to light.

Have you called on the Man who will understand?
When life's complications, to take it in hand,
Come, call on that Man when trouble is rife,
Call Jesus to sort out the fuse in your life.

He'll dispel all your darkness, the gray and despair,
And light up your life beyond all compare,
Dispersing your shadows, forgiving your sin,
While the light of his love will come flooding in.

Come, call on the Man, who created the light,
To shine in your darkness and lighten your life,
Call out to that Man because He understands,
Don't sit in the dark with your head in your hands.

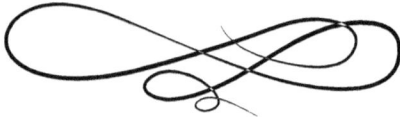

FATHER'S DAY

*Written for my grandchild who in
his early days considered Daddy
as a hero.*

Father's Day

Our daddy is big, our daddy is strong,
Our daddy is tall cause his legs are so long,
Our daddy is handsome, a nice smiley face,
His mouth, eyes and nose are in just the right place.
Our daddy's a driver, who drives very fast,
We know if you raced him you would always come last.
Our daddy's a jumper, the greatest you've seen,
The best one at jumping that there's ever been,
He takes grandma's dustbins, jumps three in a line,
If Grandma had more we are sure he'd jump nine,
Our daddy's the greatest at finding new places,
Driving his car through the long open spaces.

He does not need maps or a route to say where,
Our daddy's so cleaver he just gets us there,
When we're out and about in the fields for the day,
It's then we and daddy have fun and we play,
Football and climbing and then we have races,
Hide from each other in all sorts of places,
We can run fast but our daddy runs faster,
He says it's because he eats tuna and pasta,
Do you know what it is in our dad we love best?
The things we love most and above all the rest?
It's not that he's strongest or fastest or tall,
It's that daddy's a heart that is biggest of all.

ABANDONED MORALS

Throughout history man's morals have always missed the mark when it comes to what God is looking for. So we have to admit we need a Saviour.
There was only one perfect Man that ever walked this earth who could fulfil this role his name is Jesus. He took all our imperfection with Him to the cross and on to the grave where they were buried with him.
The glory of it all He left them there as he himself rose from the dead handing us his righteousness.
A righteousness we did not earn but was given freely through his suffering, death and resurrection.
That is an amazing love from an amazing God.

Abandoned Morals

As married you know that all are expected,
To see that each other is loved and respected,
Not exposed to the man with the wondering eye,
Or men of the world that are passing by,
But covered with dignity, honoured, respected,
As one of God's people that He has elected.

The world has abandoned God's ways and all morals
No decency practised, no standard or morals,
Perverted, they lay on our beaches exposed,
Stripped of their dignity, stripped of their clothes,
Laying on towels, on island and corals,
Sinking in quicksand's in sins murky hollows.

Now Noah's two sons, do you think got it right?
When father stripped off when as drunk as a kite?
Both walking backward they covered his frame,
When Noah got sober, imagine his shame,
In Genesis nine he admits he's to blame,
Then having repented never did it again.

Now Adam and Eve what a wonderful thing,
They could go about naked before there was sin,
But sin bought the curse, God said "That's your lot."
No more stripping is done, if you like it or not,
I will cloth you for now in an animal's skin,
But later white garments when heaven you're in.

Now those that are older, like mums and grandmothers,
We feel we must pass on this message to others,
While we failed in our youth, will you take it on board?
To walk in the way that is pleasing the Lord.

GOD LOOKS ON THE INWARD

*We did a fashion parade with the youth
group; it was fun with all the make up
and hair-do and garments we turned
up with. After it was all over we had a little
talk encompassing the following.*

God Looks On The Inward

We can spend all the time in the world
Improving our looks and our skin,
But tell me, dear child, will it cover
What lies beneath or within?

We can put all the makeup we can on,
We can plaster it thickly or thin,
We can rouge up our cheeks on our cheek bones,
And powder our noses and your chin.

We can curl up your hair with our rollers
Or perm it or plat it or spin,
We can sweat under heaters and dryers,
Putting up with the noise and the din.

We can clothe in the highest of fashions,
The latest designs that are in,
Or diet to improve our appearance,
Or starving ourselves to be slim.

Now think of the money we're wasting,
And think of the time we've put in,
With the makeup we feel doesn't suit us,
And gets thrown away in the bin.

Yes, think of the time we have wasted,
When real beauty's not outward it's in,
No matter how much are our efforts?
We must look at improving within.

You see what we need to remember,
And what we all need to embrace,
It's that God doesn't look on the outward,
It's the inward we need to replace.

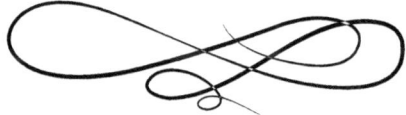

BRITISH WEATHER

This was a harvest festival when the young folk centered on the weather, the following poem was included.

British Weather

A cloudy start for this morning,
Sees a mixture of sunshine and rain,
With an occasional rumble of thunder,
But temperatures warm in the main.

By evening strong winds will develop,
From the north bringing snow to the town,
This could bring about icy conditions,
Beware of black ice on the ground.

By tomorrow we'll see that cold pressure,
Continue for most of the day,
But the long range is looking more hopeful,
As mild air is coming our way.

This will bring about warmer conditions,
Then not looking too far ahead,
You'll see crops being harvest in sunshine,
And this nation on earth being fed.

Praise God for these far emerald islands,
The mountains, the hills and the dales,
Enriched by the moods of the weather,
And his care that forever prevails.

Thank God for our variable weather,
That nurtures the seed of the earth,
He knows how to temperate the weather,
For the ground to erupt in new birth.

CHASING BUBBLES

The young people gave this message one Sunday morning, some blew bubbles; others read the following verses for me. We were seeking to answer the question of what our priorities in this life are.

Chasing Bubbles

Bubbles are beautifully rounded,
And have no beginning or end,
Floating around so light hearted,
Up and away they ascend.

As light as a feather and carefree,
They have no direction to chase,
Just go where the breezes direct them,
No purpose to follow or place.

Children will reach up to catch them,
To hold in the palm of their hand,
But, alas, as soon as they touch them,
They disperse and the bubble disbands.

There are grown-ups in life that chase bubbles,
And strive for the things that don't last.
Hoping to reach their ambitions,
Before bubble they're seeking has passed

The world waves a wand so alluring,
Blowing bubbles that float in the air,
While people run hither and thither,
To see if their bubble is there.

Now fame is a popular bubble,
Than many are searching to find,
To grasp if they can, its achievements,
In the hope it won't leave them behind.

Then power I see as a bubble,
That many are clamoring to catch,
They trample on others to get it,
Pushing others aside for that patch.

Some seek for romance never ending,
Take new loves as each marriage fails,
Breaking the hearts of their partners,
While the numbers of lovers cascade.

Another is pride, have you noticed?
How easy it is to show off,
I, me and myself is their topic,
While other's achievements are scoffed.

Some search the happiness bubble,
To continue each day without end,
Content as long as life's smiling,
And no one disturbs or offends.

I see there are bubbles out yonder,
Which hundreds are hoping to get,
It is wealth they are all chasing after,
While the poor man they seem to forget.

Then what of the lottery bubble,
Each week we see floating around,
That burst before you can catch them,
And their bubble is lost with their pound.

Can I ask you what bubble you're chasing?
Will it profit your soul in the end?
If it does not fit into God's kingdom,
You will lose out in heaven my friend.

Don't waste all your time chasing bubbles
That vanish away in thin air,
It could lead to the pit of destruction,
And you don't want to end up in there.

Remember the man that was planning
To build larger barns? What a dope,
God took his soul before morning,
Turning his bubble to soap.

Whatever the bubble you're chasing,
And want to hold on in your grasp,
When popped, it is gone, it is finished,
None of these bubbles will last.

Why not chase the things that are lasting,
That God in his love has prepared,
The things that He said are eternal,
And all with Christ Jesus is shared.

A MOTHER'S CONCERN
I was asked to write some verses
for the young to help them remember
to say "thank you" as so often they forget
may be that goes for us older ones too.

A Mother's Concern

Here I am raising a mother's concern,
With a poem I hope the children will learn,
Two little words often missing today,
Just two little words we forget to say.

Two little words those are often astray,
Two little words we would love you to say,
Two little words we would use every day,
Two little words let us hear them I pray.

Two little words that are easily said,
Two little words that are easily read,
Two little words that are missed out a lot,
Two little words that are said in a jot.

Two little words we were all taught to say,
Two little words that would brighten mum's day,
Two little words that would mean such a lot,
Two little words that are often forgot.

Two little words when you're helping them out,
Two little words that I'm having no doubt,
You could say them all day and in any amount,
Just to say THANK YOU that's what it's about.

THE FULL ARMOUR OF GOD

Written for the young people to help them understand Ephesians chapter 6. We did this as a play, performing it in church as a funeral service with makeshift coffins representing each dead solder who had not worn his part of the armour.

The Full Armour of God

The victory in battle is given to those
Clothed in God's armour when fighting his foes,
If you're lacking a part of it, do you suppose?
It goes by unnoticed and nobody knows.

Sadly we buried four solders today
Who'd not obeyed orders and died in the fray,
Part of their armour they hadn't put on,
Their bodies lay lifeless, their spirits have gone

Breast Plate Righteousness

One was a solder called William Pain,
A soldier they tell me but only in name,
When orders were given his breast plate to wear
His breast plate of righteousness just wasn't there.

Though warned of the dangers of chests that are bare
"I don't really need it", we heard him declare.
The breast plates so heavy I think I know best,
I can run faster if just in my vest.

A man with no breast plate so flimsily dressed,
Left open to arrows to go through his chest,
Shot through, the heart, O Christian beware
Don't fight for your Lord without righteousness there.

Helmet of Salvation

And now there's this feller, the one they called Ned.
Complained that his helmet was heavy as lead,
"How do they think I'm expected to see?
I'm blowed if I'll wear it I like my head free.

"So in spite of all that the Master may say,
I'm thinking of keeping it off for today,
I'll duck and I'll dive and I'm sure I will be
Safe if I'm hiding behind some big tree.

And when battles over and victory complete,
I'll take the reward when the Master I meet."
Alas, yes, you guessed it; he died in the fray,
Cause his head minus helmet had got in the way.

Shield of Faith

Now here lays the body of obstinate Billy
Careless and faithless and dreadfully silly
This solder forgot, in his absence of mind,
Went off to do battle and left it behind.

"Oh I'm not too bothered about it", he said,
"I'll get along faster it's heavy as lead."
A man with no shield? It's the enemies luck
A man with no shield he has nowhere to duck.

Never believing that's what caused his fate
No faith in his shield and now it's too late
His body lays here while his spirit waits,
Hoping that heaven will open its gates.

The Belt of Truth

When battle cry sounded its note of renown,
And armies all gathered outside of the town
Jeremy ran but with no belt of truth
His armour unbuckled and then became loose.

To hold up his trousers he let go his shield
When a dart to his chest had his destiny sealed
His destiny sealed for the lack of the truth,
Killed by an arrow, poor Jeremy Booth.

The truth we are told it will set us all free
Untruth let us down that's as sure as can be.
His funeral we are told left a sad congregation,
For the lack of the truth sealed Booth's destination.

The Sward of The Spirit

Now Jack had a sward once shinny bright,
Till it lay in his cupboard by day and by night,
Never yet used from the time it was given,
Since sent down to earth from the Master in heaven.

When battle cry sounded Jack jumped for his sward,
Away in the cupboard where it had been stored,
But, alas, it was useless all tarnished and blunt,
No use for purpose Jack died on the front.

The sward of the Spirit is given to those
Meant to be ready to fight off God's foes, Not
stored in a cupboard where nobody goes
Unused will grow rusty as everyone knows.

Conclusion
Walking with God in the fullest relation,
Depends on truth, righteousness, faith and salvation.

THE WEB OF LIES

We turned this in a production for the church with several different students; one acting as the spider. This was to show some of the devil's tactics to entice us away.

The Web of Lies

The Devil's like the spider that spins his sticky web,
Hides in cracks and crevices and feeds upon the dead,
His web is so attractive when shinning in the sun,
But mark my word, dear reader; you'll be dead before he's done.

His speech is so persuasive but folk there is no doubt,
If unaware of whom he is, he's bound to catch you out,
For he will see you coming before you know he's there,
So young folk just be ready or he'll catch you unaware,
You'll see him in the Broadway and in the city streets,
He targets the young students, in crafty tones he greets.

Spider
"Oh come into my parlour dear, how could you pass it by?
It's the most attractive parlour that ever you did spy,
It's full of dainty morsels to delight the taste of all,
And pleasures by the thousands if only you would call."

Student
"Dear sir I'm taught by others to ignore your crafty ways,
Attractive as your parlour is, I look for brighter days,
I'm told with perseverance there's a better place ahead,
Than what you have to offer and the things that you have said."

Narrator
Our Bible student shook his head; he knew his wily ways,
He knew the web the devil spins for unsuspected pray,
He knew that once inside his den he's sure to make him stay,
Once bound within that sticky web he would not get away,
And so our student fian would pass but spider unperturbed,
Will tempt a little longer as, Christians are preferred.

Spider
"But student, I have watched you and know the things that please,
And all those things you long for, my dwelling will appease,
I see you're young and handsome with many years ahead,
You have room for all this Bible bashing long before your dead,
I could give you pleasures beyond your wildest dreams,
Why, life is just beginning now that you are in your teens."

Student
"No sir, I hear your flattery that could tempt any man,
But Proverbs clearly tell us to shun you if we can,
The broad way's to your parlour, but I walk the narrow way,
Thanks for the invitation but my answer must be 'nay'."

Spider
"But dear you look so weary; did they wake you up for church?
And rack your brain all morning to do the Bible search?
Well, my parlour is so cosy you could nestle down and sleep,
Relax from all your studies and rest your tired feet,
Listen to my music, you could sing along with me,
No rules and regulations, why, your spirit would be free."

Student
"Too late to try and tempt me I know the way folk go,
That listen to your flowery words, I've heard their tales of woe,
You hold them in your sticky web; they struggle to be free,
Addiction holds them in your grasp, for this is what I see,
You tell them that the drugs they take will lighten up their mind,
But hide the devastation that your evil leaves behind.

"Yes, I've seen the evidence of all the souls you win,
And it's been told to some of us the state your parlours' in,
There's blood upon your parlour wall, and blood upon your bed,
And the web you used to tempt them in, is covered with the dead.

"I have seen my fellow students, who have followed in your ways,
And long to see them free again before they end their days,
I've seen through Christian teaching that your door leads to the grave,
I answer to the Man above, who came my soul to save."

Narrator
So, young folk, do not listen when he tempts you to do wrong,
When Satan tries to tempt you, resist, refuse, be strong,
Remember when you see his web so delicate and fine,
He's hiding in some little hole and watching all the time,
So, students, just be brave enough to answer with a "NO".
Remember he has six strong legs and will not let you go.

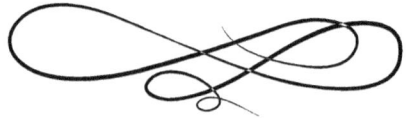

THE GOOD SAMARITAN

The world and religion go hand in hand,
while compassions of Jesus they don't
understand.
See the Samaritan touches the soul,
without any predigest makes the man whole.

The Good Samaritan

Now here is a story you'll probably know,
Of a man that was travelling to Jericho,
When robbers waylaid him, beat him up bad,
Left him half dead, taking all that he had.

There he laid wounded, life ebbing away,
With no one to help he stayed where he lay,
Then along came a lawyer, he looked from afar,
Shouts, "I'm in a hurry, best stay where you are."
I'll come back tomorrow and if you're diseased,
I'll handle your assets so mine will increase.

Then came the priest, yes he did take a look,
But what could he do without his prayer book?
He's off to a service where members await
For him in the pulpit, he cannot be late,
Beside said the priest "you must understand,
I cannot be seen with blood on my hands."

Now see a Samaritan's coming this way,
Will he stop, will he help, will he too turn away?
By the power of his love by the strength of his cross,
Bends down to help the poor man that was lost,
Bound up his wounds pouring in oil and wine,
Declaring to all that this sinner is mine.

Then putting the man on the back of his beast,
Walking beside him, his care never ceased
Then taking his invalid into an inn,
Asking his people to take care of him,
Whatever the cost he said he'd repay,
When he returned on that wonderful day.

SELF-RIGHTEOUSNESS

*Self-righteousness with good works
leaves Christ out,
and if Christ is left out all my good
works mean nothing.
Let's do what we do for the glory of
God.*

Self-Righteousness

Oh I fast twice a week and continually pray,
And I never behave in a worldly way,
I keep myself separate from earthly things,
Cause I read in the Bible the sorrow it brings,
Ask folk from the church, they'll confirm what I say,
I'm there in the week and twice on Sunday,
I help with the music and I will spend hours,
Making cakes for the church and arranging the flowers,
Turn my back on the world with its lust and its sin,
I keep myself holy and pleasing to Him.

Answer

O friend you're so separate, are you any good?
To the God who would use you if only He could,
While your down at the church whipping toppings and cream,
Pruning yourself with self-righteousness esteem,
Picture men starving and savaged with war,
The jobless, the homeless, the addicts, the poor,
And think about Jesus if He were here now,
As you read from your Bible you must have seen how,
He got involved with the sufferings of men, Displaying compassion again and again,
He was holy and righteous but never apart,
Giving to men all the love in his heart.

Reminder

Did He raise his arms in horror at the women at the well?
Or turn his back to let her spend eternity in hell,
And what about the women that was taken in a fault,
Self-righteous men condemned her but what was the result?
Did He let them stone her? No, He wrote upon the floor,
Then gently turning to her He said, "Go and sin no more."
Did you see Him in the synagogue arranging pots of flowers?
No, amid the poor and needy is where He spent his hours,
So don't recoil in horror, self-righteousness and shame,
God has given you his Spirit to go out and do the same.

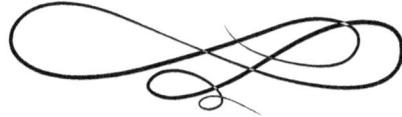

SEE WHAT A WOMAN CAN DO

*This was a scripture exam the children sat
showing how women had been used by God
throughout Scripture.
I wrote the following for the children to read
when they were presented with their prizes.*

See What A Woman Can Do

Under the palm trees is where Deborah sat,
Making decisions while judging and that.
When God gave a message through her to Barak,
To gather his army and Sisera attack.

Now Barak seemed troubled, a bit frightened too,
And said "I'm not going unless you're coming too,"
So Deborah went with him, that battle was won,
The Sisera's army was all over run.

See what a woman can do; just see what women can do,
Through trouble and strife, when she's God in her life,
You'll see what women can do.

The beauty of Esther attracted a king'
Who said for you, "Esther I'll do anything,
The half of my kingdom will not be too much."
The strength of his love for young Esther was such.

"Oh save my people", is what she replied,
"Please save my people for Haman; he lies,
He seeks to destroy to, destroy every Jew.."
Then king said, "Haman the gallows for you".

See what a woman can do; just see what women can do,
You have no need to fear for your God will be near,
And will show what women can do.

Martha and Mary with Jesus they meet,
Mary sat listening at her Saviour's feet,
When Martha grew cross and said "See all this work
Lord, tell her to help me, why should Mary shirk?"

Oh Jesus so patient to Martha He said,
"Mary is listening to my words instead,
It's not your good works that I want, but your heart
What Mary has chosen is just the right part."

See what a woman can do; just see what women can do,
Take on what you've heard and act on God's word,
And you'll see what a woman can do.

Priscilla and her husband, they had to leave Rome,
For old emperor Claudius said "No Jews in Rome,"
So they travelled to Corinth, that's where they met Paul,
Who stayed with them, worked with them, made tents and all.

Till Paul sailed to Ephesus, announcing God's word,
Proclaiming the gospel to those who'd not heard,
Priscilla went with them obeying God's call,
Prepared with her husband to risk life for Paul.

See what a woman can do; just see what women can do,
These women have shown with God on the throne
He can prove what women can do.

LEPROSY

*This was a sketch we did with the
youth to display to the church, what Leprosy had meant
to people in those days.
Each child came in with some limping
with sticks others with bandages on feet
arms and legs. Then, later freed from
their disease having met Jesus.
The following verses being read at
the end of the sketch.*

Leprosy

Leprosy is just like sin,
It's caught when we let Satan in,
Your devastation soon is seen,
And you must cry, "unclean, unclean."
The only hope for you to day,
Is pray that Jesus comes your way,
And when you're healed, please don't forget,
The day that you and Jesus met,
Remember He was most concerned,
That out of ten just one returned.

There was no cure so I am told,
For leprosy in days of old,
Imagine then the hopeless scene,
As lepers cry, "Unclean, unclean."
No cure but for the grace of Him,
Who took our case and bore our sin,
Wrath's cup He drained beyond the brim,
His one desire our souls to win,
Laid down his life that we might live,
And lepers, like ourselves, forgive.

THREE GOSPELS STORIES

THE MASTER'S TOUCH
THERE WAS A PROUD MAN
LAZARUS AND THE RICH MAN

The Master's Touch

A woman seeking Christ's salvation,
Silently in desperation,
Through the crowds she pushed her way
For Jesus healing hand that day.

Reaching out she touched his gown,
Messiah knew and turned around,
Just a touch, that touch revealed,
The Master's love, her scourge was healed.

A women's son had passed away,
The funeral should have been that day,
The Teacher saw her grief and strife,
And bought the widow's son to life.

Two blind men Christ's love had favoured,
Cried, "mercy on us son of David,"
Answered prayer, behold they see,
He touched their eyes and set them free.

If we would all but humbly cry,
Like those above the Lord draws nigh,
But those that feel they have no need,
Are lost to Him, Oh do take heed.

There Was A Proud Man Jesus Told

There was a man so full of pride,
Self-righteousness he could not hide,
"I do not gamble, do not bet,
And give away the tenth I get".

I thank thee, Lord, that I am not,
As sinful as the other lot,
I have the knowledge and the light,
To know when others are not right.

But then a tax man stood apace,
Who could not raise to heaven his face
But beat upon his troubled breast,
God's mercy was his prayers request.

God is a God, who judges fair,
For those who seek his love He's there,
But self-sufficient, men of pride,
Must humbly kneel at Jesus side.

The tax man touched the heart of God,
Who walks the way the Healer trod,
God's mercy was the man's request,
An answered prayer, that man was blessed.

Lazarus And The Rich Man

There was a rich man and, behold,
Dressed in purple, clothed in gold,
He lived in luxury every day,
Wasting all his life away.

While at his gate, not far away,
Lazarus sat there every day,
Waiting for a rich man's crumb,
Hoping he'd be dropping some.

The dogs would come and lick his sores,
No rich man came to heed his cause,
But beggar Lazarus, when he died,
Was taken up to Abraham's side.

In time, the rich man also died,
In agony to Abraham cried,
"Water for my tough I thrust,
This hellish fire is getting worse."

Alas a chasm has been fixed,
Heaven and hell they cannot mix,
On earth he had his heart's desire,
His wages now the lake of fire.

As so will be our destination,
If we take not God's salvation,
The rich man with his swollen purse,
His place in hell he can't reverse.

But hear him tell to warn his friends
It is not earth where man's life ends,
It travels on beyond the grave,
Through Christ alone you can be saved.